CRIMINAL INTERDICTION

STEVEN VARNELL

SCV Publishing, Apollo Beach Florida

For information about special discounts for bulk purchases, please contact Steven Varnell at criminalinterdiction@live.com

ISBN   0985382147
ISBN   978-0-9853821-4-8

To my mentor and lifetime supporter. Thanks Dad.

CONTENTS

ACKNOWLEDGEMENTS

Everyone in life is blessed in some way or another. Unfortunately, many of us do not always have the sight to recognize them. I am lucky to have always had the sight to know to count my blessings. To give thanks to all of the people who have made things possible in this life can be a little daunting. If I have forgotten someone who believes they should be on the list, forgive me. You are there.

This was written after decades of work in the profession. It is a profession and not just a job. A job I could have found anywhere. This profession has blessed me. I did not always agree with the course that it was taking, but they rarely stopped supporting me. I must give thanks to the Florida Highway Patrol. They gave me the platform from which to perform.

My entire career has been spent in Tampa, Troop C. A special thanks goes out to all of the Troop C, CIP teams, both past and present. It is a small, but great group.

The profession can be funny, sad and always dangerous. The last section was always reduced by my partners. I was blessed with partners who were always watching my back. I like to believe they all feel the same way about me. A special thanks goes out to each of you in the order which we were partnered; Bruce, Jorge, Joe, and Bob. Thanks.

My greatest personal support for which nothing can be possible lies with my family. I am truly blessed by and love you all; Toni, Steven, and Vanessa.

For you Draco, good suchen!

THE TRUTH OF THE STREET

1

Every year approximately 150 police officers will be killed in the line of duty within the United States. On average, one police officer will be killed every other day. Were all of these deaths caused by felonious attacks upon the officers? No, but about half of their deaths will be the result of some type of personal assault. According to statistics maintained by the FBI, nearly 60,000 officers are assaulted each year. These assaults resulted in nearly 16,000 injuries. (1) The number is staggering. I believe, without a doubt that these numbers can and should be reduced. An act of God can never be stopped, but an act of man can.

During the course of my duties as a State Trooper, I come

across other officers every day. I watch as they go through their "routine" on a stop or encounter. All of us are taught the basics in the police academies; somehow, over time we lose much of what we have learned. We have all heard about complacency. It exists at all levels of everyday life. In the profession of law enforcement, it can result in dire consequences. I do not say this to criticize other officers, but simply to make observations of their actions. I understand and have studied why many of the things we do can lead to additional dangers upon ourselves. I know we can do better. Our lives and those lives of people around us depend on us honing certain skills. My hope is to change the habits of at least one officer by the reading of these pages. As I will tell you at the end, we will all feel that self-satisfaction, at the end of the shift.

Throughout these chapters, we will cover items as basic as a traffic stop to the more difficult task (not really) of identifying a criminal. We will go through the clues they give us during an encounter that we so often miss. They tell us the things we need, but we do not listen. They show us everything required to alert ourselves, but we fail to watch. Some of the topics may seem basic to a few of you, but I believe everyone will learn something. One of the many things lacking in all police departments is training. Some outsiders believe that the training officers receive is intense and never ending. The truth of the matter is that much of it is based on tradition and not reality. The intensive training is in the beginning at the academy level. It is designed heavily to see who can take the rigors of discipline and who cannot. You only begin to learn the job once you are on the streets. Once you are on the street, budget restraints and personnel shortages usually prevent proper field training from taking place.

Firearms' training is one of the most important areas of instruction. Most agencies only qualify their personnel once or twice a year. There are many among us who can barely shoot. Every time we are on the range these same people are unable to properly load their weapon, have jams which they cannot clear, or simply fail to qualify. We will see in the upcoming chapters just how important it is to be proficient in all of the high liability areas. It is frightening to me that these same people will be my backup to purportedly drag my ass out of trouble if I ever need help. We have them in every agency, therefore the burden falls upon us to train even harder to overcome and adapt.

We are all told after a day on the range that you should get ammunition and practice on your own time. This unstructured, self-teaching time on the range, can be just as important as any formalize training you will ever receive. The agencies simply cannot afford to continually provide all of your training; therefore, the onus falls to you. I am writing this with the sole purpose of trying to share almost 3 decades of law enforcement which includes 27 years as a full time criminal interdiction officer. There are always those people who will find fault with everything. Many may disagree with the ideas I present. That criticism, if well founded, is all right with me. I am not here to tell you what the definitive answers are, but to share what I have learned along the way. I still learn new things all of the time. The officer who is locked into a single path to get to the other side will always fail if there is an obstacle on the trail. You have to always have an alternate route in order to understand the landscape. I have taught many of these ideas in classroom settings and some of

3

you may have been in one of my classes. The result of this book has been a compilation of teaching and being taught from officers throughout the country. I took this knowledge into a world of self-experimentation and practical use in the field. My father spent nearly 4 decades in law enforcement and my son is now with us as well. Getting it right means a lot to me because I will still have assets in the field long after I am gone.

Cops will always be cops. They act tough and mean sometimes, but it is a necessary part of the occupation. They are also the softest, easiest, most kind, and giving people in the world. Other than firefighters or our soldiers, who else is willing to put their life on the line for a total stranger? Until tragedy strikes in someone's life, they will only see the tough side of a police officer. Remember, the most common interactions that anyone will ever have with the police is when something has gone wrong in their life.

But with an open mind, new or old, experienced or brand new, I think you will find something in these pages which can make you a better officer. More important to me is the possibility that you change a current habit which saves your life. This sometimes occurs without anyone's knowledge, but at the end of the day, you know you did a good job. What nobler profession exists than one which protects people's property and lives? After taking care of everyone else, you complete the most important task of each day. You go home safe to your families.

WHY ARE WE THERE? - 2

The first city police services to be established in the United States was in Philadelphia in 1751, followed by Richmond, Virginia in 1807, Boston in 1838, and then New York in 1845. (2) Many people feel that justice should be handled independently by the masses without the need for an organized police force. They feel as though the police have too many powers over their everyday lives. Justice could be better served by the community itself. All those brave liberals could ban together against the evil hordes. In fact, many will tell you that it is the police themselves which are at the root of so much of the violence in today's society. Many people living in their utopias cannot tell the difference between the cops and the crooks. They believe that if you saw a problem in your neighborhood, you would organize the neighborhood against the problem. What a great idea which so many free thinkers actually believe. Now let's face the truth! How many people have ever wanted to get involved in even the smallest of issues? How many none gun owners are there who are physically stepping into the fight for this country? They certainly know how to call upon others to do the hard work. They are swift to write in their blogs about all of the evils perceived in society. The question is which one among them is willing to step up to the plate. Take a swing out of crime. Do more than run your mouth. Actions talk and the words run away to hide so they can blog another day.

There has always been and there will always be a percentage of the population who will do wrong against others. There will always be predators among us looking for their prey. There have always been a few people with the abilities required to take a stand against this type of person. Most people's life is just too busy doing other things which usually leaves us with just one option. That option has never included the above-mentioned utopia. The option which we are speaking about is that we pay others to do the work for us. Community and business people have always had other desires in mind. But they have always understood that these predators had to be dealt with. As many officers will tell you, they themselves are not always the most admired people. We have to dirty ourselves for them, but they often will have disdain towards us. They know it will be the cop who will direct them on how to conduct their own behaviors. What a shock! There are people who do not know how to conduct themselves civilly in society. It is the sheep herd mentality. All of the sheep hate having the sheep dog around overlooking their every move. The dog requires them to do things beyond their utopist freewill. That is until the wolves appear on the hill. Then the stay

6

huddled together, finally willing to obey every rule and wait for the dog to finish their fight.

Have you ever thought about the reason why there really are police officers? There are many academics who can give you the text book versions why, but for me it is just two words; Asshole Confrontation. I heard it said once in a Matt Braun novel about the great Oklahoma lawman Bill Tilghman. He said, "The good intentioned men of the world are quick to recruit others in the name of justice. But they were wary of dirtying their own hands and easily frightened. The moralists in life are seldom fighters." (3) Well said, Mr. Braun.

Most people do not have the combination of senses, integrity, and courage that are all required to be a cop. Most people cannot do this job that is a fact. It is a job for a special person. Just as it was said before, most people do not want to get their hands dirty. They do not want to face down those who need to be faced. It is a unique profession where you are given weapons. You have the requirement to make life and death, freedom or detention decisions. Any one of these decisions can affect a person's life forever. You are given a certain amount of power that no one else possesses. Yet as we all know, make one mistake and there can be hell to pay.

What other job has an internal affairs division? What other job exist where the instantaneous decisions you make can lead to your own termination, civil lawsuits, or even criminal charges? Who else do you know has to go to work each day and wear a bulletproof vest because in the course of the job someone may want to shoot you? How many people go to work and strap on guns, knives, radios, pepper gas, Tasers, a baton, and handcuffs as the defensive tools of

7

their trade. Without them, many more of us would never come home. The average person goes to work with their computers, aprons, pens, cell phones, and other common tools of their trades. They are not sure if they like you and are often afraid of your authority. I know this sounds like them versus us mentality. Nothing could be further from the truth. There are far more supporters of the police than there have ever been of detractors. Unfortunately, in our day to day dealings with the others, we do not always get to see or hear our supporters.

There are many people in law enforcement who have no business being in the job. There are so many people in the public who wish they were doing our job, but for a multitude of issues are not. It is a very fulfilling job that continues to professionalize itself more every year. Many thousands of people apply to the various agencies. Very few applicants will ever complete the process and have a career in law enforcement. Fewer yet will ever retire from the profession.

To most people, you are the cop who pulled them over for speeding or running a red light. "But I am late officer." You are the cop who only turns on their emergency lights to go through traffic lights because you are late for lunch. Or you are the jerk who arrested my friend over a little weed. The moment they need help, who are they going to call? Will it be their friends, family, or others? No, it is 911. Now it becomes, thank God you are here officer. By the next morning all has returned to normal. When they get pulled over for something else it will be, "But officer I was just going with the flow of traffic." All cops are on a power trip, right? The attitude that we face from the people we encounter each day takes a toll on you. Cynicism develops and grows inside of you. I find this topic to be so important that I will talk about it in the last chapter. You will hear the following sentence again. The job entails more than most realize and produces a brotherhood that few understand.

Many start the profession with good intentions, but the vast majority discover, for a variety of reasons that law enforcement is not for them. You have to be hard, yet soft. You have to be a strong talker and a good listener. You have to be able to think on your feet and make split second decisions. You have to be visual in your perceptions for the common things and still notice the faint clues. You have to be aggressive, yet patient. You have to be willing to tolerate what few people would throughout your career. You have to be willing to work when everyone else you know is off. You work shift work, days, evenings, relief, midnights and holidays. You have to keep yourself physically fit and mentally intact. Most people believe that cops are uneducated thugs, but actually, they are well educated. All officers today have completed high school, almost all with some college education, many with 2 and 4-year degrees, and some with masters or doctorate degrees. While in the profession, you will be required to complete courses of various types throughout your entire career. The learning can never stop.

It is a profession with no equals. The ranks of the agencies are filled with every type of person. There are ex-military, college graduates, and recruits who are very young to middle aged. They decided that they wanted to do something in an effort to help their communities. The training academies are very difficult. Most will last as long as 6 months. Most people will tell you that they would rather go through boot camp again than to go through a police academy. There is a reason for this. More police officers will be injured each year than American soldiers in the Afghan/Iraq war will. The streets can be a battle zone and it is the place we work every single day. The truth of the matter is you never can tell who will make a good cop. It is worth repeating that it entails more than most realize and produces a brotherhood that few understand.

In the end, after all of the discussions, arguments, and lectures, the conclusion remains the same. Our primary responsibility is Asshole Confrontation. The size of the asshole varies, but we are the only ones willing and ready to confront them. It is the thin blue line. It is the brotherhood. It is our job.

THE UNIFORMED OFFICER

3

The one event where citizens interact with the police most often is the traffic stop. We reach out and touch more people each day, across the country, with the traffic stop than with any other action. For this reason alone I can tell you, the uniformed officer is the single most effective weapon that exists for fighting crime. Everyone talks about becoming an undercover officer, a detective, or any position other than working the street in uniform. I have listened as investigators talk about going back on patrol in uniform as a negative action or a punishment.

The street cop will arrest most criminals. A street cop arrested most serial killers in the history of America. There is one fact that has never changed in the last century. After nearly every crime, the criminal will get into a car and drive away. That same criminal is guaranteed to be the driver or passenger in a vehicle at some point after every crime. We live in a mobile society. No longer, do most people live, grow old, and die in the same neighborhood. We are all going to drive. When trying to solve a crime we always try to find the vulnerable spot. There is always the proverbial weak link in a chain. For the criminal element it is the moment they enter a car.

Look at some of the more notorious serial killers. There was Ted Bundy, pulled over for a broken tail light. Dennis Rader, the BTK Killer, captured after a traffic stop. David Berkowitz, the "Son of Sam," was initially picked up for loitering. William Suff killed over 12 prostitutes. He was arrested after a routine traffic stop. The list goes on and on. This does not take into account the non-serial killers who have just committed a homicide. When the criminal travels to commit a crime, they carry the tools of their trade with them. When they finish their crimes, they will travel with the tools and with the elements of the crime itself. A sharp uniformed street cop will stop this person. The cop goes past the stop based on the actions of the criminal and an arrest is made. The daily news is full of wanted fugitives arrested by police after a traffic stop. They are involved in criminal interdictions.

From the Bureau of Justice Statistics, the most common reason for contact with the police is some form of traffic stop or traffic related incident. In 2005, 41% of all face-to-face contacts with police involved traffic stops and 12% involved traffic accidents. About half of all traffic stops resulted in a traffic ticket. Police searched approximately 5% of all stopped drivers during a traffic stop. Of the 43.5 million persons who had contact with police in 2005, an estimated 1.6% had force used or threatened against them during their most recent contact. (4) To some people this is taken out of context to show the injustices committed against people. What this actually indicates is that we are out there doing our job. Despite what some people try to claim, the statistic that only 5% of the drivers stopped in this 2005 study were searched is very telling. Some try to claim they are stopped and searched everywhere they go. As a person who has been pulled over by the police and you have done nothing criminally wrong, have you been searched? No probably not. There are always exceptions to the rules, but we do a very hard job very well. We have to distinguish between the innocent and the guilty during a short encounter. They both tell us everything during the stop. I hope to show you how to recognize these nuisances in the chapters to come.

What about potential terrorist? Take a look at some of the arrest.

February 2002 – I-70 in Utah, a deputy seizes $300,000.00 from an undocumented Jordanian believed to have ties to Al Qaeda. February 2002 – I-80 in Omaha, a police officer stops a car with two Jordanian's. The information obtained leads to breaking up a money laundering operation funneling drug proceeds to the Middle East. April 1995 – An Oklahoma State Trooper stops Timothy McVeigh and arrests him for driving with a suspended license and carrying a concealed weapon. He was fleeing Oklahoma City after bombing the Alfred P. Murrah building. May 2002 – Nevada State Troopers stop Lucas Helder who was identified as the mailbox pipe bomb terrorist.

August 2007 - Arrest of two University of South Florida Middle Eastern students with pipe bombs in their trunk.

These are just a few of the countless encounters and criminal interdictions being accomplished each day. Let's not forget the great cops we have on our waterways and points of entry into the United States. There are the water cops who have interdicted several possible terrorist events in and around MacDill Air Force Base, the home of Central Command for our military. There are the uniformed Customs Inspectors who stopped the Algerian man who planned to bomb Los Angeles International Airport. There was the Customs Inspector who stopped Mohammed al Kahtani in the Orlando airport. He was to be the 20th terrorist on Flight 93 on 9-11. Flight 93 was the plane that crashed into the empty field near Shanksville, Pennsylvania after the passengers courageously tried to take the plane back over. This plane was destined for The Capitol Building or The White House. With the terrorist being short one comrade, who knows what the final outcome would have been.

In earlier times and in other countries the uniformed patrol officer is called the "Preventive Police." It designates the police that patrol and respond to emergencies. The name preventive police says it all in that the first line of protection for the general public is our mere presence. Everyone tries to behave when the cops come around. We will soon learn it is with this change in behavior that we can identify the person who has excessive nervous behaviors when encountering the police.

The interdiction of criminals, fugitives, kidnappers, murders, human traffickers, gun smugglers and drug traffickers occur every day on the streets of this country. Most of us never hear of the vast majority of these events. Many will only hear about those which occur in their local area of news coverage. The average person, crook and even cop never thinks about how safe our communities are because of the uniformed officer. A lot of criminal activities are prevented simply by their presence. These preventions are never seen or recognized, but they do exist. If there was some way to account for these preventions we would all be amazed by what is accomplished just by having a marked patrol car driving in an area. There are programs around the country where the local police will park a marked unit at a location and leave it. The crime in that location generally goes down even though there is no officer in the car. Just the presence of the patrol car alone deters criminals. Many people owe their lives to the street cop who just happened to be in a certain place at a certain time. Their presence prevented their property from being taken, personal harm from occurring or even homicide. However, because these events never took place, it is not possible to account for them. Every cop out there knows that they have saved lives by simply driving down a street.

Everyone loves statistics, so let's use them for a moment. How many times has a cop been told after a traffic stop, "Don't you have anything better to do than to stop me for ….?" Fill in the blank. We have all heard it at least a million times for every violation somewhere. A scene from the Kevin Costner movie "The Untouchables" always brings the question clear to me. There is a scene on a bridge in the front part of the movie where Costner is leaning on the rail of a bridge. Sean Connery walks by as a beat cop and sees Costner throw a piece of paper into the water. When Connery questions Costner of his actions, Costner says the same thing.

Connery - You want to throw garbage? Throw it in the goddamn trash basket.

Costner - Don't you have more important things to do?

Connery - Yeah. But I'm not doing them right now. Do we understand each other? (5)

If you would like another answer to the question you can always provide them with the statistics from the National Highway Traffic Safety Administration. There are over 6 million traffic crashes each year. Approximately 40,000 people will die in the U.S. from traffic crashes alone. Almost 3 million people will be injured with a financial cost of about $230 billion dollars. (6) Yearly, there are fewer than 10,000 murders. Statistics now show numerically which one is about four times more important. However, to the victim and their families, the loss is the same. You cannot devalue one over the other. A loss is a loss. But to everyone, cops included, it is the homicide investigator who gleams all the accolades while the uniform cop just does his job. Though one can see that I am bias when it comes to this issue, I can still honestly tell you I have nothing but respect for the investigators. They are doing a tough job, but everyone forgets where they first learned the tricks of the trade. It was as a uniformed patrol officer working the streets. It is like the offensive linemen of the NFL. Most of us know very little about them, but can tell you everything about the touchdown makers. Few touchdowns would ever be made without a good offensive line. The uniformed patrol officer is the best source of everything that is happening on the street. They can tell you who is doing what, where, and with whom. They are the criminal interdiction officers.

PROACTIVE PATROL - 4

There are many definitions for a good cop. In my opinion, a good cop is aggressive. They seek out their activity. They are proactive. They do not sit and wait for someone else to radio them their next assignment. You are on patrol and observe someone waving to get your attention. You stop to see if you can help the person. This person tells you that people in the area are driving too fast and are not stopping for the stop signs. They then proceed to explain your plan of enforcement to deal with this activity. They instruct you to park in an adjacent driveway and enforce the aforementioned violations. Is this actually going to happen? I think not! We sarcastically laugh at the thought of this scenario. But, by the same account, waiting for a civilian dispatcher to tell you what your next assignment will be is exactly the same thing. Go on patrol and stay aggressive. The dispatch center should be interfering with your proactive patrol.

While on patrol, a felony call comes out. Everyone is breaking their necks to get there. At the same time while on patrol, you see a person leaning into a car. The two exchange something. The person then drives away and the other person walks off looking around suspiciously. In all probability you just witnessed a felony drug purchase! Most uniformed officers drive by and know what is happening, but fail to react. Why? There certainly are enough reasonable suspicions to conduct an investigative interview. Besides, the pedestrian is probably going to run when you approach. The driver is going to be very nervous if you pull him over. These actions are some of the responses that we will be watching for. Their actions will add more to substantiate your observations.

My first partner and I would collect information where the most crimes had occurred. Working at night, we knew where the drug holes were located. We would go to these areas and park on a dark side street. Using binoculars, we would stand at the edge of the street and watch as cars would stop at the end of the block. When they finished, the car would drive past our location. The drivers would not be able to see our marked patrol cars in the dark. We would follow them out of the area and conduct a traffic stop. Only one time was the driver or passenger not holding drugs. On this occasion, the driver had a $20.00 dollar bill in between his legs. He just had not yet decided to buy the drugs, but he would have on the next approach. We would then watch to see where the dealers were going to pick up their drugs at the time of the sale. Some people call it their "bomb". It is the larger stash which dealers will keep nearby. When a sale has transpired, they will remove from the stash the amount of drugs sold. In this manner, they may not be caught with drugs on their person. We would then drive to their location and stop. Of course everyone would run. Some of them were caught and arrested. Most would slip away in the night. We would then go and seize their stashes. The intelligence gathered would be given to street crimes units. We made a lot of arrest and were always in uniform with marked units. An aggressive patrol officer can seize more drugs than most narcotics detectives have ever dreamed of getting.

You must know the laws of your state. You must seek out the simplest of violations. Some may call them petty, but their enforcement is your job. You do not write the laws you enforce them. This knowledge of the law gives you more abilities to reach out and touch. It opens additional avenues to conduct a stop. The more quality stops you have, the more arrest you will make. Remember, Ted Bundy the serial killer, was arrested over a tail light. There are so many factors of safety, especially with a new officer. In addition, it takes a new officer time to comprehend everything. With time comes the experience. The problems arise from the type of academic and field training each officer receives. I know there are field-training officers who are inexperienced. They are training new recruits with only 2 or 3 years of experience themselves. Are these the veterans we need to train our recruits? How much experience can possibly be shown to the new recruit? How much information is retained and what is lost without repetitive actions. We are all taught many good techniques, but then we forget them without regular use. Every stop should be performed as if it could be the best stop of your life. It certainly could be the most dangerous. There are so many factors to consider each day. It is impossible to stay completely focused on the job during your shift. Every officer has to have that mental sharpness each day to stay focused. I have always gone back to the fatal errors made by police officers to help keep myself focused. Here they are for you to use as your daily guide:

a. Your attitude – The failure to keep your mind on the job. We each have different circumstances taking place in our personal lives. There are illnesses, divorces, financial issues, problems with children, etc. If you are not maintaining your attention on the job you must do something about it. Take a sick day or an annual day off. Make sure you discuss issues that can affect your performance with your zone partner. Some will think that these issues are no one else's business. However, you depend on each other for personal safety. When someone else's well-being can be determined by how you react, it is their business. Withholding your problems is fine for an office job. On the streets, you can get someone hurt. They can watch over you more closely. This is something most of us forget. We are completely dependent on one another.

b. Tombstone Courage – Yeah all right, we all know you are a tough guy. Do not hesitate to wait for back up. When I first came on, I was told you do not call for backup unless you were already in a life or death situation. What a stupid philosophy. Call as soon as you believe backup should be there. That extra sense we possess is usually right on the money. When the hair on your neck stands up, the radio is pressed.

c. Rest – We all have been guilty of this. Our bodies need rest. Any fitness trainer will tell you the big three issues for health are exercise, nutrition, and rest. All are equally important. Your mind and reactions are not as sharp when they are tired. In today's world of overtime and off duty, remember which job comes first. Most agencies have maximum hours allowed requirements for on duty and off duty employment. How many of us see officers work a shift all day and then have to be on duty all night. They are dangerously tired. They become inattentive and in no hurry to do anything, but sleep. They may have made a couple of dollars to put in their pocket, but at what cost.

d. Bad Positioning – This applies to everything from the placement of your car to your personal placement. Our positioning in various situations will be discussed later. But remember, if possible, your car should be well off the road. You should always maintain a lot of distance from the violator. Make a passenger's side approach and keep everyone in the vehicle.

e. Recognizing Danger – This will also be discussed later in detail. We mentioned earlier that we do not always hear and see what has been said and done. We are good at seeing the large issues, but usually we will miss the small clues. Brake lights or turn signals are still on after the stop, breathing, behaviors, etc. You will find this fault frequently in officers because they are moving too fast. Motor cops are notorious for having activity requirements. If you want to stay on the squad, you will produce activity. All this produces are unsafe practices and sometimes leads to excessive punishment to many drivers. How many tickets are you giving each person? You have to slow the pace of the stop down to recognize what is happening.

f. Hands – The two things that will usually lead to us being

21

injured or killed are the hands. Watch a person's hands. You do not have to stare at them, but always be aware of them. The hands are the weapon which is going to strike you, push you, or draw a gun. We will see later through scientific studies how attention to the hands produces a faster response to danger. Watch the hands because they also indicate a person's level of nervousness. When the adrenaline begins to pump, the hands will shake.

g. Relaxing Too Soon – Never completely relax in any type of encounter. Unless you have stopped your mom, the person is a complete stranger in every way. Their history, their temperament, or their intentions are unknown. I know you have to relax during your shift. This can occur while on patrol. By paying attention to yourself and your surroundings, you will discover how quickly you elevate or deescalate your senses.

h. Handcuffing – All too often, we do not handcuff a person that should be secured. It is all right, go ahead, and handcuff to detain. Do you have a reasonable suspicion that the person has or is going to commit a crime? If yes, then handcuff them. If it is later determined the person is not going to be arrested, you can take them off. Remember (f) above. You are much safer having the one thing that can cause you the greatest harm secured. In a profile of officers killed, as examined by the FBI, other officers stated they would have reacted sooner than the victim officer had. This is a lesson that many newer officers fail to comprehend. Hesitations can cause you harm.

i. Search – A bad search is no search. Always search a person well. Always search a vehicle thoroughly. Pat downs are different. Can you ask to pat down anyone? Yes, you can. Can they refuse? Yes they can. Should your internal alarms be going off if they do?

Yes they should. Do not forget to crotch a person if you are searching them. Make sure if you do, it is a person of the same gender. Only 4%-8% of offenders questioned ever felt they were thoroughly searched. 70% said they had never had their groin area searched; therefore, the groin area is their preferred place to conceal a gun or contraband. With the opposite sex, you can use the back of your hand to complete the pat down.

j. Equipment – Goes without saying. Keep your equipment clean. Test daily those things that are supposed to be tested i.e. Tasers, handcuffs. I like an old Navy SEAL saying that one is none and two is one. If your gun jams, you have none unless you carry a backup. The same goes for two knives, handcuffs, and several handcuff keys.

We could probably all add to this list. Creating anything to this list which has a safety focus is a bonus. Thinking ahead and always studying the situation is critical. Once you have determined that you know all there is to know about law enforcement, you have committed a grievous error.

We should all be in some type of physical fitness program. You do not have to be Charles Atlas, or maybe more of you would recognize Arnold, but get out and do something. If you do not like to run, do some type of strength training, walking, swimming, or biking. Look at the Officer Down Memorial Page website and you will see several officers each year who die from on duty heart attacks. (7) It is about taking a proactive approach to the job. Your personal appearance can have consequences or benefits. Outside of probably living longer, a sharp, well-kept officer displays a greater air of authority. I am not talking about arrogance, but attentiveness to the job. We all know those arrogant self-centered officers. We never want to try to immolate them. Examining several cases where officers were assaulted and murdered, the criminal stated they felt that they could overtake the officer. Sometimes the criminal stated the officer did not respect them. They were too easy going. All predators in life seek out the weakest prey by appearance. If they had to choose to attack an officer, who would they attack. The officer, who is overweight, has a sloppy appearance, and their equipment is dirty. They have missing equipment on the belts and stains all over their uniforms. What do I mean by missing equipment? I know you have seen the officer who does not wear their radio outside of the car. The officer who has forgotten their flashlight during a low light traffic stop. Or do you think the predator is going to go after the officer who is physically fit, well-groomed, sharp equipment, good stance and posturing. Sometimes none of it will matter, but many times, it will. It goes back to the one word I have used for my family, friends, and opponents. Choice; we all have choices in everything we do. Some will refer to it as freewill. Only you can choose which choice you wish to pursue.

Keeping the list of fatal errors in mind, let's take a look at the FBI's study on Law Enforcement deaths. (8) Their studies show that the mistakes made by law enforcement that contributed to their demise was:

- Failure to wait for back-up
- The failure to draw their weapon when the time was appropriate
- Tunnel vision when dealing with more than one individual
- Failure to keep people in their car

24

- Their vehicle placement after the stop
- Failure to immediately control a known suspect
- Mental planning of different scenarios

We see these issues and refer back to the fatal errors. We will see all of these repeatedly in the pages that follow. We can examine each of these topics. We can discuss them, think about them, and see what we can do to avoid them. What can I do to make myself a more safety conscience and efficient officer? When you see your partner make these mistakes, bring them up to them tactfully. Remember, there are very few sheep in this profession. Sometimes you will do better by diplomatically talking things out with them rather than by being blunt. But it needs to be talked about. This officer may be your back up one day. You will not want them to make the same mistake when your back is turned and your life could be on the line. We have all been guilty of the mental errors and tactical mistakes. It is inevitable and unavoidable. But, any reduction in the number of these mistakes that we make can save lives.

THE TRAFFIC STOP - 5

There is one area that is rarely practiced once we have left the
training academy. It is the practice of various tactics for a traffic
stop. I know you have made thousands of them and believe there is
no need to review the strategy of a traffic stop. I say you are
dangerously wrong. We have made so many traffic stops; I believe
most of us have become complacent. We try not to use the
terminology; however, most officers view them as routine. I see so
many errors committed each day by officers in traffic stops. Most of
the agencies will study the causes of patrol car crashes. After
collecting the data, they always review what can be done to avoid
them. We always discuss the dangers of guns, yet rarely talk about
the dangers of cars. I like to put it this way. You are in a regular
sized room when you are given a choice. The event will happen and

you must stay in the room. You can lie down or seek cover behind the tables, but it is your choice. Option A is someone on the outside will fire a gun at the window of the building and into your room. Option B is someone will drive a car at 70mph into your room. Given these mandatory options, we would all accept Option A and probably be left unscathed. Options B will in all likelihood, lead to us being injured or killed. A motor vehicle is the true deadliest force. We constantly practice to defend ourselves against the persons in the cars we have stopped. Rarely do we practice tactics to protect ourselves from the cars going past the stops.

We are on patrol on any road system of America in a marked patrol car. You see a violation ahead and you decide to take action. We have always known that one of the most dangerous situations for law enforcement is the traffic stop. There exist dangers as you pull out into traffic to make a stop. There are the additional dangers inherent with the overtaking of the targeted vehicle. Then there are all of the dangers that exist after the traffic stop. With time and repetition, all of these actions seem to fade in importance. Because there are problems at every level of the stop, they should always be in the back of your mind. Not to frighten you, but to keep you from becoming complacent. Because of the speeds involved, an interstate system is by far the most dangerous place to work. There is good reason why pedestrians are forbidden and there are minimum speed limits on an interstate roadway. How many people are actually driving the speed limit of 70 mph? We can say the actual number is rather low. Most people are driving much faster. At 70 mph, you are traveling at approximately 105 feet per second. The standard perception-reaction time is 1.5 seconds. Therefore, by the time you react, you have already traveled over 157 feet. You will travel almost half the distance of a football field before your brake response to avoid a collision has begun.

You are working patrol and decide to conduct a traffic stop. Just prior to the stop you enter the tag number into your in car computer, if you have one. You start watching the occupants in the car. You are taking note of their activities. Has anything about their behaviors changed? Are there passengers in the vehicle? Are the passengers looking back at you? Is the driver changing his driving patterns or committing any additional traffic violations? Is the driver watching you obsessively in the rearview or side view mirrors? I have always preached to anyone who would listen. Never just, race up to a car and immediately stop them. Give it a moment to see how they are going to react as you are driving behind or near them. This is the start of your encounter.

You should already be taking a mental inventory of what you see such as: bumper stickers, air fresheners, or maybe a rental decal in the side rear window. They will place bumper stickers such as police or firefighter unions, American flags, or patriotic symbols on their cars. They want you to believe that they are on your side so you will not stop them. Excessive air fresheners should attract your attention. Have you ever placed a dozen air fresheners in your car? We have also seen cards of Jesus Malverde, "El Rey Guei de Sinaloa." He is the patron saint of smugglers. Even as common today as Malverde will be Santa Muerte, the saint of death. If you are not familiar with either of these characters, you should be. They are very visible in the smuggling trade as both tattoos and figurines. When the car pulls off the road, what happens? It sounds simple enough, but a lot of additional information can be obtained at this point. How long does it take them to stop? Are they using the turn signals? Do all of the lights on the vehicle work? Are there any changes in the occupant's behaviors? We ask ourselves this question again because the behaviors may not change until they are actually pulled over? Often times you will see a passenger fake being asleep. Should your level of awareness be increasing? Yes.

The violator moves to the right side of the road and stops. For the safety of everyone involved, be sure that the location is right. When I say right I mean is it as safe as it can be. Is there plenty of shoulder or is it next to a ditch, guardrail, or some other obstacle. If it is not a good location, then it is your responsibility to move the stop to a better location. You have to choose the location for the stop, not the violator. How many times have you seen a police officer talking with a violator against a wall? It sounds so simple, but the "routine" is overriding their common sense. How often, while working on the interstate, have you heard the sound of a vehicle hitting the rumble strip on the shoulder? That vibrating tire sound always draws your attention, especially if it is behind you. You always curse the driver in your mind because that could have easily been on top of you. Get off the road. Get all the way into the grass if you can. Have the other driver do the same if possible. Remember, the vast majority of people you pull over have only committed a traffic offense. You brought them to where they are; therefore, it is up to you to keep them safe until you have completed the stop. This last paragraph carries a special meaning for me. On 9 June 1989, my field-training officer Lt. Benedict J. Thomas was walking back to his patrol car. He had stopped to check on an abandoned car on I-75. As he reached his driver's door, another driver accidentally drove off the road and onto the emergency shoulder. I lost a friend that day I will never forget. It is for "BJ" I can tell you to get your car completely off the road. Handle your business as far from traffic as is possible.

The stop takes place and it turns out to be a bad spot. Give the violator instructions via your PA system or approach partway to explain where you want them to move too. Tell them "I need you to drive past the guardrail and pull completely onto the grass." "I need you to drive to the next parking lot on your right and stop inside of the lot." Be specific, otherwise they will use their own judgment, which is why you are having them move in the first place. They are only responding to the lights in their mirror. They are not giving any thought as to where the best place to pull over will be. Many people have never or rarely ever been pulled over. The safety factors of the stop are up to you to determine. Do not pull up alongside of them and talk to them out of your window. Some of you chuckle because you have done this or have seen this performed many times.

What about your positioning in the car? At the time of the stop are you still wearing your seatbelt? Do the policies or specific training requirements of your agency dictate when you can take off your seatbelt? In my opinion, your seatbelt should have come off at the time your emergency lights were activated. By the time the cars come to a stop it is too late. If someone intends to do, you harm you now have immediate avenues of escape. If the person suddenly speeds away after the stop, all you have to do is put the seatbelt back on. How many times have you tried to get out of your car and you were still wearing the seatbelt? How many times has the seatbelt been caught on a piece of equipment on your utility belt? What if the person suddenly brakes hard while you are stopping them and you do not have on your seatbelt? You must maintain plenty of distance. The discussion of distant is forthcoming; however, your car should be just far enough away that they still know you are pulling them over. I know of a specific case where the officer had tried to pull over a known killer, but positioned his patrol car very close behind the subject. The criminal saw this action and slammed on his brakes. The patrol car actually crashed into the rear of the bad guy's car. The killer immediately exited and killed the officer as he sat in his car. The officer was probably temporarily stunned by the action and was never able to respond.

Another important aspect of the stop will be the brake lights and turn signals of the violator's car. Are they still on after the stop? I mentioned this before, but they can be a very telling action. If they are still on, ask yourself why? Who would sit in their car with the turn signal continuously clicking? Why would they sit in the car with their foot on the brake? Most people would place their car into park. Did you see the backup lights flash as the car was being placed into park? These are all very important questions because it shows the occupants are preoccupied. We will see this again later when it comes to the all-important statements about audio occlusion and mental preoccupation.

The driver stops the car and it is at a good location. You pull up behind them and stop. Most officers will stop somewhere between a few feet to one quarter of a cars length back. I do not understand why this is such a standard practice for officers across the country. The distance should be at a minimum of two cars length and preferably more. I have seen where after the stop, you would have to back the patrol car in order to read the tag. You will know the distance is appropriate when you have to hike in order to reach the violators car. Most officers stop very close so they do not have to walk so far. It is so hot outside. It is so cold outside. I am so tired. We all know about excuses. I try to teach that even at a traffic light you should be stopped about a cars length or more away from the traffic in front of you. In the event that you need to pull out quickly, you can. Also, if you are struck from behind, you may not have to suffer the second impact with the car in front of you. This is a habit I practice even in my personal car. You never want to be trapped in a position with no options. There are no negatives to the distance you place between the cars. Stopping very close to other traffic has no positives. We are practicing safety, so let's take a look at it.

Think of it as being on the firing range. The closer you are the better shooter you become. The more distance created, the longer you need to set up to be accurate. How many times have you stopped a car only to have the driver immediately exit the car? How surprised were you? How vulnerable were you? Had you even taken your seat belt off? Think of the complete disadvantage you had while sitting in the car if the driver you pulled over had the intentions of doing you harm. Think back to the true scenario I described that cost an officer his life. If you were stopped too close to them, they only had to walk 15 – 20 feet to shoot you at point blank range. Even if they walked half way or 7-10 feet, how hard of a shot, was this going to be? Even for an untrained shooter, you will probably be shot.

Most police involved shootings occur no further than 21 feet (81%). 58.8% of all police shooting occurred from 0 to 5 feet. In fact, the FBI's "Law Enforcement Officers Feloniously Killed in the Line of Duty" research from 1994 to 2006 showed that law enforcement officers failed to hit their assailants 69.4% of the time. (9) When I first started at the academy, our last 6 rounds of a fifty round course, was from the 50-yard line. This was not a practical shooting course. Over time and with the examinations of police involved shootings, the course was modified to a distance not greater than the 25-yard line. Still nearly half of our qualifying shooting is performed from the 15-yard line or greater. There is no reality in these distances. Most police shootings will occur in less than 3 seconds with multiple shots required to bring down a suspect.

Instinctive shooting is a style of shooting that needs to become a required practice with every department. If your department will not allow it, then you will have to practice on your own time. There will be no sight picture, sight alignment, breathe, trigger squeeze in this training. You must draw and fire as fast as possible. It must be done safely and with accuracy. You must teach yourself to hit where you are looking. You must have the target sighted in without taking the time to look at your sights. You start the technique slowly. You must teach yourself the motor movements involved which are required to begin placing the action into memory. Slow and easy while gaining speed with practice. We all know the one area of the body that when hit, turns out the light instantly, is a head shot. As it was once taught to me, a shot placed between the upper lip and eyebrow will sever the stem producing an instant kill. Of course, the shot does not have to be placed exactly in a person's face. Practicing to hit a tighter group with this technique will assure you a faster hit than your opponent will. If you ever have to use your gun, then it is a life or death situation. It will be your life or your death depending on how well you train. I already know the thinking behind most agencies. They will say "have you seen the way that many of our people shoot? There is no way we can teach this in the field without taking the risk of someone being hurt." The answers are easy. As a firearms instructor, I say stick to your own rules. If someone cannot learn to properly handle a weapon, then fire them. If not, then let them be someone else's backup. I do not want to be hurt because there is someone who is incompetent watching my back. What other profession which faces life and death decisions keeps incompetents? Most others will be washed out.

Force Science Research Institute describes itself as; "studying the science & human dynamics behind deadly force encounters". (10) They have a very interesting site, which you can go to on line and read their articles. They will also provide you, free of charge, with emails to show you where some of their research is currently. In Transmission #134, they conducted a fascinating study entitled: How your eyes can cast your fate in a gunfight. They experimented with both elite seasoned officers and fairly new officers. The experiment was conducted where an officer was advised they were going to encounter a possible deadly threat. The test was to see where the officers were looking at the first sign of the threat and how fast they responded. It was found that an officer's performance can be impaired or enhanced by where their eyes and attention are focused in the midst of a deadly encounter.

The study began when a subject became irate in a lobby area. After a moment he spins towards the officer, usually drawing a handgun. Sometimes he would spin and have a cell phone. They

34

provided the officers with special equipment to determine at all times where their gaze was focused upon. Here are some of their findings:

First, the elite officer spent significantly less time assessing the situation before drawing their gun. On whole, they drew "well before the assailant began his pivot." Most drew early and "held [their gun] at chest level before aiming." The rookies tended to delay drawing until about a second after the subjects turn.

The elite officer shot before the assailant got his round off 92.5% of the time, beating him by an average of nearly 180 milliseconds (ms). The rookies shot first only about 42% of the time and on average lagged behind the attacker by more than 13 milliseconds. Responding "very poorly," the study says, the rookies essentially "reacted to his attack, rather than being ahead of him as were the elite officers during every phase of the encounter." The rookie's final saccade or rapid eye movement, especially among those who missed when they fired, "occurred at the same time they tried to fixate the target and aim," the study reveals. At that critical moment in the last 500 milliseconds, the rookies in a staggering 82% of their tests took their eyes off the assailant and attempted to look at their own gun, trying to find or confirm sight alignment as they aimed. "This pulled them out of the gunfight for what turned out to be a significant period of time." Also noted was "On a high percentage of their shots, the rookies did not see the assailant as they fired," contributing to inaccurate shooting and the misjudgment of the cell phone as a threat.

The researchers pose the possibility that the rookies' training may have contributed to their poor performance. They were taught pistol craft "similar to how most police officers first learn to shoot a handgun: to focus first on the rear sight, then on the front sight, and finally on the target, aligning all 3 before pulling the trigger." Somewhere across their training, practice, and experience, the successful elite officers had learned what essentially is a reverse process: Their immediate and predominate focus is on the weapon carried by their attacker. With their gaze concentrated there, they bring their gun up to their line of sight and catch their sights only in their peripheral vision, a subtle sight glimpse.

This study says in more terms that are technical what I was saying a moment ago. The standard practice of sight picture, sight alignment, needs only to be taught initially to recruits for the basics of shooting. The real shooting lessons should be taught up close and without the use of sights. Military elite forces are taught this technique while law enforcement never trains in the methodology. Maybe you can see why we lose most of the gun battles with the bad guys. We miss nearly 70% of our shots against an assailant. Because the shootings happen so close and so fast, there is no time for aiming. Most police officers are not prepared for this type of confrontation. Instinctive style shooting is the answer to this problem.

Edged weapons or even any blunt weapon, when possessed by an offender, deserves the same attention as a gun. The old standby rule we were all taught was the 21-foot rule. Stay at least 21 feet away from a person who has picked up an edged or blunt weapon. You should be able to draw and fire your weapon before being struck by the assailant. Studies have shown they were wrong. In a new study, one researcher found that an individual can cross 30 feet in 2 seconds and suggested that the person could travel 70 yards before succumbing to injuries created by an officer's firearm. (11) According to the FBI, "There is sufficient oxygen within the brain to support full, voluntary action for 10 to 15 seconds after the heart has been destroyed."(12) Can you draw and fire in this time frame? You had better give it some thought if you cannot. Do you ever try to fast draw your weapon? Practice this at home with an empty and safe weapon. If you have not drawn your gun when someone is squaring off against you with any type of weapon, you should re-evaluate your tactics. Remember the fatal errors from above include not drawing your weapon when danger is recognized. On this note, I know officers who will not pull their gun out in situations when others would. The why to this statement can be varying. Many supervisors are very confused in their interpretation of use of force. Too many people see the drawing of their weapon as a use of force. It is only a use of force if you have to pull the trigger. Prior to that moment, it is a show of force. The other reason is the officers become hesitant over the fear of lawsuit, arrest, or the loss of job. It is pounded into their head that if you do this or that, you will be held liable. It causes many officers to hesitate instead of reacting. You cannot afford to hesitate when confronting a potential life-threatening situation. Agencies have to pull away from worrying about financial responsibilities versus their personnel's own welfare.

Have you ever practiced drawing your gun from the front seat of your cruiser? Because of the various styles of holsters today, you may not be able to get your gun out. Try it with both the seatbelt on and off. Also, think about the placement of other weapons you may carry on duty. Are they locked up in the trunk? Are they locked in a gun rack in the passenger's compartment? Are you wearing a backup weapon? Have you ever tried to draw the backup weapon while sitting in your patrol car? What about having another accessible weapon in your car? Take advantage of them only if it is allowed by your agency. As you can tell I believe strongly in the preparations to every event which I may be faced with. Fatal errors tell us all about lack of mental preparations. Even though the actual practice could appear to be physical, you are playing the situation out in your mind.

Many officers are killed or seriously injured each year during foot pursuits. I know we want to catch the bad guys. How many times you have heard on the news about an officer being ambushed by the subject they were chasing. There is no reason for you to leave your car and the subject's vehicle to run after someone alone on foot. Again, cover needs to be provided by back up officers. You will find that the subject will sprint away from the scene, but quickly runs out of steam. When their adrenaline rush ends, their tank will be empty. Slow your pace down and be methodical. You can still overtake the suspect because you will be able to move over greater distances without exhaustion with a slower pace. Also, you can change positions with other officers who are fresher. If the call allows for the utilization of a K-9, you will not want to have people running all over the place and contaminating the scene. Just in my area alone, over the last few years I have been to two funerals for officers involved in foot pursuits. You always have to think about your own safety versus catching a petty criminal who will eventually be caught anyway. Wait for the backup, establish a reasonable perimeter, and let's take these thugs into custody safely. Let us also remember to be sure to pay close attention to the subject who runs from you. How many times have you had someone flee from a scene; however, moments later there is very little physical descriptive information given to other officers. If the subject is dangerous, by not slowing down and following safe procedures, you have made it even more dangerous for the responding officers. Instead of instantly recognizing the perpetrator, they will have to investigate people who could be the suspect.

Remember earlier when we spoke about mental planning? It is part of the seven deadly mistakes by officers. It also falls under the 10 fatal errors category. This is a good time to discuss what we mean by mental planning. I am on patrol and stop at a traffic signal. I look over and see the front of a convenience store. I imagine in my mind what I would do if I saw someone run from the store with a weapon. I just witnessed a robbery. What will I do next? Do I have to think about it or do I just react. If you have played this scenario out in your mind a hundred times, you will react. If you have never thought about it, you will hesitate. You will have to think about each action you take. The same goes for traffic stops. I make mental plans for various situations that can occur in each stop. As the car is stopping, I will watch and think about various possible scenarios. If this happens, what would I do? If that happens, what would I do? Mental planning is a rarely used tool in our profession. It carries with it as much value as the physical training. What do you think the bad guys are doing all day? If they are in jail, they are mentally planning. If they are at home devising some criminal act, they are mentally planning the occurrence and so should you. When I am out on a stop, if it has come to a point where I have the driver out of the car, I am mentally planning. We will discuss when the driver should be out of the car later. However, I am standing there watching the subject and planning my reactions to various possibilities. If this guy breaks bad on me, what would I do? I usually picture a throat strike or other action I know will incapacitate the subject quickly. Another axiom, which is taught to military Special Forces, is the best defense against a physical attack is to avoid it if possible. If a confrontation becomes physical, strike as hard as possible, with whatever force is needed and back away. Separate yourself from the attacker and give yourself the chance to take a stronger defensive action with one of your weapons. But, if the opportunity does not present itself, you strike as if your life depends on it. Anytime a subject physically attacks an officer, it has to be perceived as a life-threatening event. None of the defensive tactics practice in the world will prepare you for the real thing. If you have been in a real fight and not when a subject is just trying to get away from you, the violence will shock you. Practice deadly response tactics to defend your life.

The same is true with situational awareness. Be aware of your surroundings at all times. I already know that this not completely possible all of the time. But just like your traffic stops, everywhere you stop should be considered. As you pull into a parking lot or an abandoned area to work on reports, be aware of the area. When walking into restaurants or convenience stores, do you survey what is going on inside before entering? Do you sit at a restaurant in a place of advantage or disadvantage? Wild Bill Hickok was killed while sitting at a table with his back to a door. Recently in Washington State, four police officers were shot to death while sitting at a table and working on their computers at a coffee shop. Situational awareness is everywhere you go on or off duty. You should park in an area where you can leave easily and it is well lit.

The area where you park should have a clear view all around. This is so you will not be surprised if someone approaches you. Remember, with the technologies that exist today in a patrol car, like in car computers, it causes us to stare at the technology all of the time. Be aware of your surroundings at all times.

THE INTERDICTION STOP - 6

It is true that the more stops you make the more opportunities are presented to you to make an arrest. However, contrary to the thoughts of many, there are different qualities of stops. What do I mean by quality? Within the first minute of the stop, you should recognize whether to send them on their way or take the stop further. The signs will appear to you almost instantly. You have to stop a variety of vehicles, but you also have to play the odds. Let's assume you are operating stationary radar. You see an elderly couple that you clock speeding. Behind the vehicle is a rental car with two younger males who are also speeding. To play the better odds you would stop the car with the two younger males. Does this mean that the elderly couple has not committed a crime? No, but the odds are greater that the two younger guys have. Additionally, you should never try to stop more than one car at a time for safety reasons. We see multiple car stops all the time by officers who are solely stat driven. Some will argue that this is a pretextual stop. We will cover pretextual stops later. However, it does not matter what was in your mind before the stop of a vehicle as long as that vehicle has committed a traffic violation. They were both violating the traffic code and are each equally susceptible to being stopped.

If all you do during your shift each day is work speed enforcement, then you are eliminating most criminals from your stops. There are a percentage of criminals that will speed all of the time, but most will not during their criminal activity. The stops must be for a variety of reasons. Again knowing your traffic laws is critical. Many stops are for what some will call BS stops. Remember that you are paid to enforce the laws of your state and community. I have never looked up a violation in a law book under the chapter of "BS violations." What you need for a vehicle stop is probable cause. If there is none, you leave it alone. I have always said to throw it a seed. It will grow and come back another day. Never put your reputation on the line with any gray area stops. Make it a good stop for a violation which you can articulate and you will always be fine. I know there are officers that will follow a car, mile after mile trying to find any reason to stop them. When you first observed the car there was no probable cause for a stop. You caught up to the car to look at it and the occupants closer. You run the tag and everything appears all right. Turn around and find another car to stop. Many cars with different types of criminals are driving by your location all day long.

You are sitting in the median or the shoulder of any roadway

43

USA. Are you hiding or out in the open? Many of us will hide so we can surprise traffic offenders. The target vehicles approach and you clock them at the last second before they have a chance to slow down. You want to see them before they see you so they cannot stop what it is they are doing until it is too late. This can be a great strategy if all you want are traffic violators. I say the interdiction officer should be out in the open most of the time. This allows numerous things to happen. First, if you are hiding on the opposite side of an overpass monitoring traffic, almost all of the traffic that comes over the crest will react to you. They will break, grab the steering wheel, change lanes, etc. When you are out in the open, generally only certain ones will change their behavior. When people are traveling down the highway, they will have tunnel vision. All they are going to notice is the area just in front of the car. On the interstate systems, most people just stare at the car in front of them or the lane they are traveling within. The furthest down range people will watch is about a quarter mile. Cops always want to hide in order to catch traffic violators when they could do just as well by not hiding. You are looking for the clues that appear from people who are not doing anything very wrong. You have to look twice at a car that is driving at or below the speed limit, but slows when the driver sees you.

Criminals always know they are criminals. Criminals always react to cops. It is up to you to recognize them and their actions. They know you are there to catch them. When they are committing, have committed, or are about to commit a crime, no matter how large or small, seeing you causes a reaction in them. These reactions are what we seek. It takes a little practice and patience, but it will pay off. In the open, you are watching traffic approach. You see their actions before they see you. What you want to see is their actions when they do see you. You will know when you see them. Speed may start to decrease or the front of the car will take a nosedive if they brake too hard, regardless of whether or not they are speeding. If you are in the median and they are in the inside lane, they may move to the outside lane. They may or may not signal the lane change. Subconsciously, they want to move further away from you. What was once a relaxed driving position becomes an intense one. They will grip the steering wheel with both hands. They may not look at you when they drive past. If there are two people in the car, do they look relaxed or have the thousand mile stare as they drive by you? Some may look away from you, others may rub their head, face, or play with their hair. These are the same nervous reactions you may see in a personal interview. It will be reactionary, subconscious, and without thought. There are many different reactions from people. Not all of these people are criminals when they do react to your presence. Some people are nervous by nature. Others could have gotten into trouble recently, no matter how minor and have a reaction to the sight of the police. This will be shown to be very important later on. In the minds of those people who are guilty of something, they are being looked at or stopped by you for the worse thing they have ever done. They are not thinking about their speed, faulty equipment, or any other traffic violation. In their mind, it is because they stole the clothes from the store at the mall or some other criminal act.

A car approaches your location and slows down. They activate their turn signal and change lanes to the lane furthest from your car. They drive by you and are sitting straight. You noticed as they approached that they were leaning over on the center console. They go by you and grab the steering wheel with two hands. When you first recognized them, they had their left wrist lying across the top of the steering wheel in a very relaxed position. They now look tense. If they are concerned about you, they will be watching you after they have passed your location. They will want to see what your reaction to them will be. They will be watching their side view mirrors and/or rearview mirrors. They will not be paying attention to their driving. The cruise control will not be set because they braked a moment ago and their speed may continue to fall. They may drive outside their lane of travel, tail gate another car, or suddenly create distance to the other traffic directly in front of them. A good location for performing this type of patrol observation is just before any type of curve. You can really see how worried they are after passing you as they try to negotiate the curve. It does not have to be a sharp curve. A shallow curve will highlight their inability to stay in the lane. But there will be a change in behavior. You have to be alert and watching the entire series of events. You may recognize some of the events and miss other parts. It is only important for you to see some of these behaviors that drew attention to the driver.

To better explain the last section to you, let me provide an actual case summary to you. While working one night on US27 (a four lane highway) in Polk County, Florida, my partner and I watched as two cars approached. They were driving under the posted speed limit. They were the only two cars in sight. The second car was tail gating the first. As they approached us, the driver of the first car hit the brakes. The driver of the second car had to brake hard to keep from hitting the first car. This tells me that the first driver saw us in the median and braked. The second driver was doing what most drivers will do. They had tunnel vision on the rear of the first vehicle. A young man and woman occupied the first car. They were in a new car and it appeared to be a rental. The second vehicle was older and occupied by two males. We could see this because when working at night, we will sit in the median perpendicular to the roadway. Our lights are on and shining across the lanes of traffic. You will want to do this so you can see the occupants in the car as they travel past you. They will react to you the same, but without the lights, you will not see it. Be sure the lights are not shining down the lane of traffic because the drivers could be temporarily blinded. We are stopped in the open on a long stretch of road.

As the two cars drove past our location, we already had probable cause to stop the second car for following too close. My partner and I were in two separate marked patrol cars. The second car continued to slow down until they were separated by several hundred feet. As we proceeded north, I saw the first car drive completely off the road and onto the outside-unpaved shoulder. This occurred at a small curve. Why did this happen? Because the driver of the first car was watching us in his rear view mirrors instead of the road. As the grass, dirt, and rocks flew into the air, I proceeded forward to the first car. My partner stayed with the second car. Why? Because they were the only two cars in sight on the road; therefore, you should be questioning yourself why the second car did not just pass the first car. Remember we are on a four-lane road and they are traveling under the speed limit. We both believed at the moment that they were traveling together. But why would they be in separate cars, especially a rental car if they were in fact traveling together?

We coordinated between ourselves quickly. I told my partner to stop the second car when he saw the emergency lights of my car behind the first vehicle. I told him if his targeted car stops away from my stop location, he was to move the stop to a position behind mine. At least in this fashion, we could provide immediate backup to each other. I activated my emergency lights and stopped the rental car. I watched as my partner activated his emergency equipment and stopped the second vehicle. The second vehicle, by this time, had slowed so much that there was now at least a quarter of a mile between us. I exited my car, but waited to approach as I watched my partner's actions. A moment later, I watched the second car and my partner drive directly behind my car. I now approached the car I had stopped.

My vehicle stop had a young male driver and young right front passenger female. I saw in the back seat a fast food bag with food boxes in the rear floorboard. I also saw that there was a single red rose in one of those plastic containers on the rear seat. You would get the type from a convenience store. I asked for the driver's license and registration to the car. He produced both. The driver explained they were going home from Miami, Florida. He stated that he was trying to spend some "quality time" with his girlfriend so he thought he would take her to Miami for the day. I then heard my partner yell "gun! Let me see your hands!" I looked back and saw my partner with his weapon drawn and pointing it into the car. I told the driver of my car to give me the car keys and he complied. I ran back to cover my partner. We removed, handcuffed, and secured the two occupants of the car he had stopped. The passenger had reached for a handgun in the glove box as the driver was trying to get the registration. He immediately released it as my partner drew down on him.

Why did I take the ignition keys from their car? It was my belief that they were traveling together. If they tried to escape or chose to run us over, he could not without the keys. We removed the gun and I saw a fast food bag with food boxes. They were from the same restaurant as the bag in the first car. I do not believe strongly in coincidences. I returned to the first car carefully. I asked if they knew the people in the car behind them. They said no. We utilized a K-9 on the exterior of the rental and he alerted positive to the trunk area. A search of the trunk produced a couple of kilos of cocaine. A satchel was found in the second car with money and cocaine residues. The couple from the first car was arrested for trafficking in cocaine. The guys in the second car were arrested for conspiracy to traffic in cocaine. We followed the route they had traveled and found the fast food restaurant where the food had been purchased. The fast food employees identified all of the persons involved. They stated how the four of them had ordered all of the food together. However, the employees had to place two of the four meals into separate bags because they were in separate cars. The outcome for everyone involved was guilty in state court. The two subjects from the second car were tried additionally and later in federal court.

Can you see how it all comes together? What if I had been alone that night? I do know which car I would have stopped. I probably would have chosen the rental. If they were traveling together and had anything illegal, it would be in the car that none of them own. We will talk about rentals later. I can assure you I would not have stopped both of them. I also would have been extremely careful about the stop if I had felt that they were traveling together. If the second car had stopped, I would have ordered him to wait down the road at the next business. No search would have taken place without backup.

What quick points were noticed about the first car before the arrest? First were their nerves. Then you think about the story. Does it make sense to you? The drive to Miami is 6 hours one way from their home. There are no clothes in sight and they are eating fast food on the go. There is nothing romantic about a cheap convenience store flower. They bought the flower to try to add credence to their story if they were stopped. All of that was gathered in the 30 seconds I had with them before the events in the other car occurred.

Their physical actions while driving may not be probable cause to stop them, but the results of their inattention to driving will be. Failure to drive in a single lane, following too close, speed, driving too slow, and failure to signal a lane change, could be a result of their carelessness which you could use. If there are no clear violations, leave it alone and wait for the next one. You pull out to look at a car that has driven by you. You do not have enough information to conduct a stop; you just want to look at the car. There was something about the car or its occupants that did not seem right. Maybe you had a funny feeling, so you pulled out after them. Trust in those feelings. Your body responded to something it recognized that you just couldn't explain. I have found many younger officers who will ask; "Can I do that?" Sure, you can. You just want to look at the vehicle. You are not going out to stop the vehicle on a hunch. You are trying to confirm or deny the feeling you had. Keep all of

50

your activity on high moral ground and no one will ever be able to harm your profession.

We were discussing earlier about pretextual stops. It used to be that a pretextual stop was illegal. However, the Whren decision from the United States Supreme Court states that pretext is no longer a negative factor. The only decision to be made is if there was a legal reason to stop the car. I remember in the past, a stop had to be for a reason that you would commonly stop people for. I have seen good cases thrown out because of the violation committed was minor, but it was a violation just the same. Unfortunately, the officer had never or rarely used the particular violation. Defense attorneys would claim you stopped their client because of this or that reason and only used the traffic violation as an excuse. In other words, a pretextual traffic stop.

Now you can think whatever you want before the stop as long as the reason for the stop is a legitimate violation. You were somehow not supposed to have any fore thought about the vehicle you were stopping. No one cared about your educated hunches based on years of training and experience. To summarize the Whren decision it says; that when a police officer observes a traffic violation, they automatically have probable cause to stop the offending vehicle and to issue a citation or a warning to its driver. With probable cause thus established, any incriminating evidence of the traffic violation or any other criminal activity found by an officer in plain view within the stopped vehicle could legally be seized and used as evidence in court. The Court also rejected the argument that traffic stops used as a pretext for obtaining other evidence should be abolished, noting that such pretext would be impossible to ascertain.

In the final analysis the Court ruled that as long as a traffic stop was made following an actual traffic infraction it was reasonable by definition. (13)

I think this is a good place to bring up racial profiling. Briefly is about all I think this subject deserves. Simply put, if you haven't heard it too often already, do not do it. Crime is an equal opportunity occupation. If one was to only choose one race to enforce the law upon, you would be missing out on the greatest majority of crime. Just about every officer, regardless of his or her own race, has been accused of some type of racial profiling. I am sure it has occurred at times somewhere in this country, but I have never witnessed it. It is an extremely rare occurrence, but a very regular complaint. I had a fellow officer who once told me he had a racial profiling complaint filed against him. The officer who is white said the defendant, who by the way had cocaine on his person, stated the only reason he was stopped was that he is Russian. Everyone has a beef with someone and some have more beefs than others do. Don't do the crime if you cannot do the time. The very accusation of this in order to muddy the water in a clean well has always disgusted me. It is usually in an effort to get off from a crime you have committed. Punish those who violate the rules and leave everyone else alone. It is the typical excuse of all excuses, which tries to damage a proud profession. There are groups of people in each race which are more prone to do different crimes. The Mexican drug trafficking organizations control the vast majority of drug transportation into the country. Is this a negative statement towards Mexicans? No, it is simply the facts. Transportation around the country may be by any race once it travels from its storage hubs which are close to the border. Blacks predominately distribute crack cocaine. Are all crack dealers and users black? No, they are not. Whites predominately carry out the prescription drug trade. Are whites the only distributor of the illegal prescription drug trade? No, but more importantly do you see the common thread? All drugs are transported, distributed, and abused, by all people across the entire color spectrum. The population of the area in which you work can cause one group to be predominating over the others in the makeup of your stops. We will see this later on when we discuss marijuana grow operations in Florida. But never is any one race solely responsible for any of the many drugs that plague this country. It has nothing to do with driving while black, brown, yellow or green. It is just another desperate attempt to escape taking personal responsibility for your actions. It is simply a crutch to lean against so you can pass the blame. I know I was transporting 10 kilos of cocaine, but the only reason I got caught was because I am .... It is always the same crap, but it is just from a different asshole. The fact of their color did not cause them to be arrested. It does have everything to do with the fact you are an asshole on society. We did what we were supposed to do and confronted the asshole. Remember, it is why we are here.

I see it all of the time. A car drives by with tinted windows. The window is lowered slightly and you cannot see inside. Because the window is lowered, you know they are ventilating. But ventilating what? The weather is bad, it is raining. Maybe it is cold or very hot. A person drives by you with a newer car and their window is down. You have to ask yourself why? Can you justify a reason why you would drive like that? Always put yourself in the car you are observing and determine if what you see makes sense. Does this guarantee that something is wrong? Of course it doesn't. Not everyone behaves the same, but for most of us, it is very similar.

You are working on a section of highway and a car drives by. The driver exhibits many of the things we have talked about thus far. He approaches you and changes his behavior in the vehicle. He drives past you and commits a minor violation. All of his behaviors have attracted you to him. Because of the traffic violation, you conduct a traffic stop. Is this person a criminal? Not necessarily, but it is time to find out. Usually they are not criminals. Most of the time there will be no reason to even search the car after the stop. So why did they behave like that? It could be any of a number of things. Maybe they are just nervous around the police. Maybe they had gotten into trouble in the past, but still fear doing anything else wrong. Maybe they have a bad driving record and know that if they get just one more ticket it will cost them their license. Many times, I have found it was a person driving with a suspended license. Other times they had warrants for their arrest. Sometimes they had drugs or guns. The point of the matter is just because they exhibit all the signs of a guilty person, there may still be nothing to the stop. Unless it is a known criminal you are stopping, you must still be professional and courteous until their actions call for adjustments by you. Their behavior will dictate your actions.

While patrolling on side streets, we have all seen a driver react in some way that has attracted our attention. You will see people at a stop sign waiting to pull out, but then they see you drive by in the direction they had intended to travel. How do you know they were? Their blinker is on or it comes on when they see you. They have their tires turned slightly in the intended direction. They have every opportunity to pull out, but they do not. You have to be saying to yourself; "Why not?" You are watching them in your rearview mirrors after you drive past. You begin to slow, but they suddenly turn and go in the other direction. Have they committed a crime or violation? Not unless the turn was prohibited. They have done enough though to cause you to be turning around quickly. Does your quick action cause them to take any additional reactions that appear evasive? You must remember, maybe they were not from the area and confused. Maybe they changed their mind as to where they were going. But maybe they wanted to stay away from you.

If they suddenly drive into a parking lot, but still have not committed a violation, go to an area where you can stop to watch them. If there is not an immediate area that you can travel to, then go down the road and position yourself where you can watch their exit back to the road. If they do not come out for a while, drive by again and see what they are doing. If they have exited and walked into somewhere, do not spend any more time on them. Often times, they will travel back out to the road and in the other direction once they believe you are gone. If they do, see if they have changed drivers or see if there is any reason to stop them. If there is none, move on to the next person. This is all proactive patrol. We spoke of this earlier about being aggressive in your patrol. The more often we can remove a criminal from our roadways, the better off our society will be.

Inclement weather, be it rain or snow, leads to some additional dangers. I will not make regular traffic stops in the rain. Other drivers cannot drive very well when the weather is good. When it rains or snows, the dangers of out of control vehicles greatly increase. Why take the additional risk? My advice to you is if you feel that a stop in these conditions are necessary, due so with extreme caution. But be sure it is necessary. I learned my own lesson one day while working overtime. It was a bad place to be stopped and it had just finished raining. We were required to have a certain amount of activity while working overtime. I had to approach the driver's side because of a ditch. While standing there, I was grazed in the back with a side view mirror from a passing vehicle. There I was, standing on the driver's side, the roads are wet, and traffic is traveling past me from about 3 feet away. One of the cars was watching me instead of the road. He drifted towards me and traveled past at about 1 foot of distance. I went home and said never again. And I have never again put myself in that predicament.

One more bit of information on inclement weather. Uniformed Immigration and Customs officials usually man the border checkpoints. The Border Patrol checkpoints on the United States border with Mexico are going to be inland. Generally, you will find the checkpoints about 60 miles inland. Because of their nexus with the border, all of the roadways leading away from the border will be covered. As illegal persons and contraband make it across our porous borders, they will soon thereafter be transported by vehicle. Sounds familiar from earlier and you will hear it again. All criminals enter into a motor vehicle and are therefore subject to our scrutiny. When it rains in the border areas, because of the traffic hazards involving motor vehicles and wet roads, the Border Patrol will often close the checkpoints. No traffic will be stopped and inspected. The smugglers know this too. They will make a dash for the heartland of America as soon as the rains come. As an interdiction officer, you watch the daily weather reports from the border areas. Determine how long of a drive it is to your area and for how long has it been raining in the border area. For instance, when I see it is raining in the Texas Valley, I know it will be about a 26-hour drive for the smugglers to reach Tampa. If it rains for 2 hours, I will give and take a little time. I will definitely want to be looking for vehicles from this area in the next 24 through 30 hours. The vehicles may not be Texas plated, but I will pay attention to people with the appearance of driving nonstop around the clock. This strategy will pay off with due diligence and patience.

Rental cars have always been the vehicle of choice. As we mentioned earlier, if a person is arrested in a rental car he will not lose the vehicle through the forfeiture seizure laws. The occupants using the car for nefarious reasons will often not be on the rental agreement. It will be rented to a third party. They will use a third party or a stolen credit card in order to rent the car. Sometimes, they will have their own associates working at the rental car company. They are often late on their returns or have someone continuing the lease. The car will not belong to them, but they will do things to personalize it. Why would you do things at your own expense to a rental car? Things like apply window tint, attach a club to the steering wheel, and personalize the key chain. You have your own car, but you pay hundreds of dollars a week for a rental and continue renewing the contract. Again, would you ever do this? Would you rent a car for someone else and put the risk on your credit card? 99.9% of the population will say no.

If you stop a rental car and the driver is not on the rental agreement, you have several options. Be sure to examine the rental agreement for the "due in" date. Check the mileage of the car and compare it to the mileage on the agreement at the time of the rental. Is the mileage excessive? Was the car due in days ago? Call the rental company and verify that the rental agreement was continued. Is the car being damaged by the third party with actions you would not do to your own property? Call the rental car company and explain there is a non-contractual driver in the car. The person who rented the car is not present and you have the following things taking place with their property. The rental car company will often times advise you they are sending a tow company out for their car. You can then advise the occupants to exit the car and find an alternative form of transportation. Again, you have to ask what you would do in a similar situation. If the totality of the circumstances does not make sense to you, then you must take the stop further.

THE APPROACH - 7

The passenger's sides approach is without question the best approach for your safety. How many times have you walked up to a car on the passenger's side and scared the driver? They are watching their side view mirror for your approach on the driver side. Everyone expects you to walk up on the driver's side. For this reason, you should not go there. Never act in a way they would expect of you. Keep them a little off guard and do the unexpected. Again, you need to control every aspect of the stop. There are more dangers for the officer at a traffic stop than in almost any other action you can take. Standing on the passenger's side, your car, and its distance provides a barrier from oncoming traffic. The violator's car gives you some more protection from a direct impact. From the driver's side of the car, you are limited on what you can see. To observe the inside of the car, you have to move beside the driver or in front of them by the A frame. Neither of these places is at all safe. Not even having the experience of being a police officer, how much confidence do you have in the other drivers around you? There is a reason why we have always been taught to drive defensively. How many distractions take place in today's technological society? When you stand at the driver's side of a car, consider the fact that the traffic is going past you from about 3 feet away. Do you really believe you are invincible? I have almost been a victim of this position and refuse, unless no other options are available, to be there again. People's eyes are attracted to the bright emergency lights and want to see what you are doing. The same philosophy applies to a bug zapper. They will always have a tendency to steer their car in the direction of the lights, all be it unconsciously. Is this really where you want to be standing?

From the passenger's side you can see the front seat and the complete right side of the driver. When they retrieve paperwork from the glove box, you can see inside of it. I have found people who will still hide contraband in a glove box, but deliberately place it on the left side. They expected you to be on the driver's side of the car where you cannot see the left side of the glove box. The entire box comes into view and from a much closer position when standing on the passenger's side.

Usually if a driver intends to do you harm, he will have a handgun. Even if he is left handed, the gun will probably be in or near his right hand. If he expects you to approach on the driver's side, he will turn to shoot you. You will have nowhere to go from the driver's side approach. If you move away from the vehicle, you will be in traffic. If you stay in place, you could be shot. Turn to run, you

60

can be shot and run over. To shoot you is nearly impossible utilizing his left hand because of how far he will have to twist. From the passenger's side, you can see the action hand in advance. Staying behind the side door post, means the driver has to reach up and over the seat to shoot at you. It will be a difficult maneuver for anyone to do successfully. As we have already seen, having your focus on the hands gives you an advantage if you are prepared. It has always been said that if they really want to kill you they will. They know what they want to do and you do not. Good tactics and mental preparations gives the advantage back to you or at least puts you on a level playing field.

Here is some good data as it was provided in an FBI Study. (14) Offenders' carry a weapon with them when?

- At work 30% of the time
- At home 42%
- Just out traveling around 56%
- Traveling with a destination 62%
- Involved in a criminal activity 74%

This shows if you stop a criminal, the odds they will have a weapon are high. If it is a gun, most will have it on their person followed by under the seat and on the seat next to them. Considering the locations that they will most likely carry a weapon, you can observe all of them from the passenger's side of the car.

Contrary to what has been set in our mind, the greatest dangers are traveling towards you from behind. Driver distractions mean death and injury to the patrol officer. We always think and prepare for the criminal element in the car we stop. If you look at your actions taken at the stop, many are for everyone's protection

61

from other driver's. Having the cars drive completely off of the road or into a parking lot. Stopping your vehicle, several car lengths back. A passenger's side approach. These are some of the actions that you took to protect everyone, including yourself, from the next car approaching from behind. More officers will be killed or injured from other drivers at the scene of a stop than will be assaulted or killed from the occupants inside the car in an average year.

You make the traffic stop and the violator pulls over in a good spot. They stay in the car as you stop at least two car lengths back. You have already run the vehicle tag and it shows a valid registration. The driver appears to match the description of the registered owner. Your seatbelt has long since been removed and you immediately open your driver's door. You turn on your handheld, exit and approach on foot. Some will tell you that you should go backwards behind your car and circle around to the passenger's side. Others tell you to go forward from this point. The reasons vary. Some say you should never stand in between the cars. This is true. But we are not going out to stand around we are simply passing through. It is also dependent on whether it is daylight or night. If it is at night, we have several additional steps to make at the stop. One will be to turn on your spotlight and shine it into the passenger's compartment. The other is to have your flashlight ready. The flashlight is another piece of equipment that falls into the one is none two is one category. Few of us ever think about it until you are working at night and your flashlight quits working. I like my large, vehicle charged, Department issued flashlight. It serves not only as a light source, but also as a weapon. "But you have never been trained in the use of a flashlight as a weapon!" I hear you already. If you are about to get your ass beat and the flashlight is the first weapon in your hand, defend yourself! I also carry an additional light on my utility belt. This is the light I am going to use to search a car if the circumstances arise.

In my opinion, if the stop is made in the daylight, I am going to approach the passenger's side of the car straight on. I will exit and move forward before moving over to the passenger's side. This is where I want to conduct my business. If the stop is made at night, I will exit and pass around the rear of my vehicle and approach the passenger's side.

In the daylight, they can see you through their rearview mirrors. There is not as much surprise if they see what you are doing. There is no need to walk the extra distance involved. They will often still be caught off guard. You will see them roll down the driver's window and start to look for their driver's license. Also during the day, I may approach as if I was going to the front driver's door, but turn at the trunk to the passenger's side. At night, once the spotlight has been positioned on the vehicle, the occupants cannot see you or your approach. If you pass between the cars, they will see your shadow as you break the beam of light. Therefore, you can take the extra steps required to walk around the back of your vehicle. They will never be able to see if you are approaching the drivers or passenger's side. But the approach will always be on the passenger's side.

As you complete your initial approach to the vehicle, you turn and walk back to your car. As you do, every couple of steps, you should look back over your shoulder to make sure all is the same with the occupants of the car. You get back to your car and initiate whatever action you intend for this driver.

In today's modern patrol car, there can be so many distractions. Technologies change constantly. I remember not having a handheld radio and hand cranked windows. You would roll down the passenger's window and hang the microphone out the window. Then you would turn on your outside speaker so you and the violator could hear all of the radio communications. Added to that was the cross draw holster and drop pouches for ammunition. There was a manual choke in my first Chrysler patrol car so I could idle the engine at a higher speed when I was out on a call. You rarely heard anyone call for assistance. But if you did, you knew that trooper really needed help. The actions that we would take against people who resisted was also different than today. I would hear the old timers say that they would never take crap from anyone. Back then, rest assured they did not. But today things are different. That philosophy of no back up was as stupid then as it is now. Sometimes when I think back, I am amazed we were not all killed. People are different. The respect for the uniform is not what it once was.

More safety issues arise once you are back at your vehicle. More than likely you have a computer in the car. If it is possible, you can stand at the passenger's door and complete your work. Most of us will climb back into the driver's seat. The new computers in many units are not very adjustable to allow a 180-degree rotation to work on both sides of the car. Remember situational awareness. Be aware of your surroundings all of the time. Do not just sit there with your head down in the computer. Stay alert and cognizant of the actions of the vehicle's occupants. If they are fidgety, stop and give them your full attention. Again staying at least two car lengths back gives you the added distance and time to react. I will regularly look behind me as well. You never know when someone will stop behind you even if it is to ask a question. I do not like surprises. Whenever someone on the road surprises you, you should use the experience as educational. Think about how it happened and what you could adjust so it would not happen again. Just imagine if the someone you never saw or heard was with the person you have stopped and they intended you harm.

There are always situations that occur that cause for a change in plans. What if the driver pulls into the median? Am I still going to make a passenger's side approach? No, but I will pull further than the violators car into the median. This will still give me some tactical advantages by having my unit between us and several car lengths back. I will then have to approach the driver's window. Remember the greatest threat to you is approaching from behind. At least with the driver's side approach from the median you have eliminated one of the threats to you. A passengers approach now is too dangerous. What if the vehicle has nontransparent tint? I can tell you a large percentage of your arrest will involve window tint. Criminals like to be hidden. They feel a sense of security behind the tint. They can easily see out, but you cannot see in. Everyone remembers the DC Sniper case involving John Allen Muhammad and Lee Malvo. The first thing they did to prepare their vehicle for the assaults was to tint the windows.

In Florida, there is a window tint law. It requires a minimal visible light transmittance for the side and rear windows. There is no tint allowed on the front windshield. The only exception is the small strip at the top of the window above the AS1 mark. This is a federal standard mark on windshields that can be found at the bottom of the natural tint line.

There is an additional statement in the law that gives the specific ratings (In Florida the law states 28% on the sides next to and adjacent to the driver and 15% for the rear windows) and states "or makes the windows nontransparent." I have used this one word, nontransparent, before in court when I did not have a tint meter available. I have also used the word nontransparent to describe the window tint on the vehicle which I observed which led to me to conduct a traffic stop. I have had defense attorneys ask me if I thought it was subjective on my part to say the windows were nontransparent. My answer is always no. Either you can see into the car or you cannot. This is the meaning of nontransparent. One person will not see any more than another will if you cannot see into the interior of the car. I have never lost the argument in court. I will also utilize a tint meter. It is the one piece of equipment I use many times daily. If you see a rental car with window tint, it was not done by the rental agency. Rental car companies will tell you that they will charge a person's credit card to have it removed from their vehicle. It is the person inside seeking a false sense of security. Many people will now use the disposable tint. It is very dark, but will peel right off the window without leaving any residue. Each state will have an approved list of acceptable tint meter devices. I encourage everyone to get one any way they can. As you will see it will pay for itself quickly. Again know the laws in your state.

There are several ways to approach these vehicles. Approaching a vehicle with window tint carries its own set of challenges. As you exit and approach the car, the driver will usually roll down his window. You can now see the driver in his side view mirror. If not, request the driver to do so by you using a hand motion of manually rolling down a window. Speak loudly and request the driver to roll down all of his windows if you cannot see into the car. Because the front window should be clear, before a stop on a tinted car is made, you can try to see through the back window. You will only be looking through a single tinted window as the light from the front silhouettes everyone inside. From the side, if you try to look directly into the vehicle, you are trying to see the area between the driver and passenger windows to the opposite side that are both tinted. You may not be able to see anything. Always try to observe from the side and at an angle from back to front. This way you are again using the clear windshield to make out silhouettes. Sometimes a driver may tell you his windows will not roll down. Have the driver open the doors. Once you can see all is clear inside the car, take up your position on the passenger's side.

The next thing you will want to do is have the driver close all of the windows except for the front passenger's window. If for uncontrolled reasons you are on the driver's side, have them keep that window down. The reasons for this will be clear later on.

THE INITIAL CONTACT - 8

We have identified the violation and conducted a traffic stop in a safe location. We exit our patrol car and approach the vehicle. It is now time for our initial contact. Now is the time to utilize our entire God given senses. There is a lot to do for the officer at the initial contact. Take your time. Go through the steps slowly. Allow yourself the opportunities to thoroughly complete the contact. You make contact with the driver and explain the reason for the stop. Already we are going to work in many areas seeking any reason why this stop should be expanded or released. We make a quick observation of the vehicle interior and the driver. If there are passengers in the car, we also want to visually examine them for any signs of nervousness. Do we see anything illegal or unusual? Is there residue on the clothing of any of the occupants? Remember they will often times fill the bowl of a pipe, roll a joint, or make a blunt while driving. When they do, they will always spill part of the contents somewhere.

Explain the reason for the stop and request the drivers required information according to the laws of your state. I like to explain the reason for the stop as soon as possible. Several things can occur in the beginning. Remember earlier we talked about this and now is where it can help. In the mind of the person being stopped, they are being stopped for the worse thing they have ever done. In your mind, you are pulling them over for a simple infraction. Your guard may not be as high as it needs to be. He knows he just robbed a convenience store. You have no idea about the robbery. By explaining why you stopped them immediately will let them know why they are being pulled over. It helps to clear the doubt in their mind. Initially you may even see them relax a little. At this time, they may even become friendly or apologetic with you.

If the person really is up to a criminal act, you can pretend to be the naïve traffic cop. They put their guard down a little and yours becomes heightened. You have recognized some small actions or behaviors which have put you on alert, thus giving you a little bit of extra time in the event something happens. You are mentally prepared with situational awareness. I will usually tell them at this time I will just be giving them a warning and sending them on their way. "You all will be out of here in a moment" is something else I will commonly tell them. They may not want to take any actions against you if they believe you will release them in a moment. The second advantage is if a person is a member of the criminal elements, they will not as often argue with you over minor things like a light out, window tint, or speed. You represent authority or the

69

enemy in their eyes. They do not want to be in your company any longer than they have too.

Also, when I first approach a vehicle, I like to immediately look at the steering column and keys. Is the steering column busted or is there a single key in the ignition. Maybe the steering column has been covered with a towel. Any of these things can be significant. Of course we know if the column is broken, the car may be stolen. If there is a towel over the column, they may be hiding the fact that it is stolen. If there is a single key in the ignition, why don't they have any additional keys? Everyone carries a set of keys for their home, cars, etc. It may not mean anything or it could mean that the car is not theirs and they were only provided with an ignition key. The key to open the glove box and trunk is somewhere else. This should draw your suspicions. Many officers have let stolen cars leave because they are only focused on getting their activity. Slow the progression of the stop down.

While the driver is looking for their license and vehicle paperwork, watch everything closely. Continue to look around and watch for bulges or other items under any of the occupants clothing. If there are any passengers in the car, what is their behavior? Are they engaging with you, helping the driver locate some of his required documents, or staring straight ahead? Look into their face at their breathing rhythm to see if it is normal or fast and short. Can you see their carotid artery pumping blood rapidly? Can you see the front of their shirt jumping because of their pulse? Watch the suprasternal notch, which is the soft indention at the base of the throat. When they are nervous, there is a release of adrenalin as the heart rate increases. Their insides are preparing for the flight or fight syndrome. This increased heart rate will cause the suprasternal notch to pulse. All of these are very important factors in determining your next steps.

I once had a car stopped for speed and following too close. I had the driver at the side of my patrol car. I knew I wanted to search the car after noticing he was a little nervous and his trip plan did not make any sense. His car had the appearance he was living in it. But most interestingly was the fact that his spare tire was lying in the back seat. I had asked him to step out of the car after my backup units had arrived. I was watching him closely as I got to the question of why his spare tire was in the back seat. You could clearly see every beat of his heart via his suprasternal notch pulsing. His nervous system was starting to go into overdrive. He said he had too much luggage in the trunk to keep the spare tire there. Does this sound about right guys? I know how we like to pack heavy for a week trip by ourselves.

I said he had an unnatural trip plan. He told us he was going to Colorado for a week from Miami, Florida. He stated he was going on vacation. He wore a wedding band and was traveling alone. Even with a girlfriend and not a wife, how many significant others would like to see you go across the country on a vacation alone. In and of itself, is this anything? Not much, but added to other indicators and it will be. How long would it take to drive there and back again? Does he have enough time to complete what he has told me? Would you not just put your excessive luggage in the back seat and leave the spare tire in the trunk? Do you see how it all adds up? Is this similar to any of your vacations? If it does not make sense to you than it probably is not correct. He had 513 pounds of marijuana in the trunk.

While you look at the passengers, watch their movements and listen to the statements of the driver. Is he nervous? Are his hands shaking? This is very visible as he gives the documents to you. Are his behaviors normal when compared to everyone you have made contact with in the past? Is he too talkative, has a nervous laugh, too friendly, aggressive, talks to himself, or angers quickly? Together with other issues any of these actions could be an indicator of guilt. If the driver cannot find his paperwork, but never opens the glove box or center console, make a mental note of it. When he says, "I must have left it at home or in my other car". Ask him if the paperwork could be in the glove box or center console? See if there are any changes to his behavior when you ask the question. Is there a hesitation which indicates thought or an instant direct answer. Ask him if he would mind looking in the glove box or center console because it is paperwork they are required to possess when operating a motor vehicle. They usually will go ahead, open these areas, and look for the paperwork. This will give you the opportunity to see inside. If there really is nothing there, you just satisfied your curiosity.

Familiarize yourself with marijuana and other drugs. I know this sounds simplistic. I can hear you saying, "What are you talking about? I know what marijuana is!" I am talking about studying the plants to understand all of the various differences. Learn how to grow marijuana and you will learn things about sexing the plants, the items one needs to grow marijuana, and the fact it has seeds and stems that will not look like any other plant. The chemical makeup of cocaine HCL and how it is converted to crack. The chemicals needed to make methamphetamine. What each of the drugs looks like because of these changes is based upon the cooking process. Include in your studies all of the various types of paraphernalia. When you see a gun you will know it is a gun. However, will you recognize some of the components of a bomb? Do you see why it can be important to understand all of these categories? Study all of these subjects and become a better interdiction officer. It is not always drugs that we seek or even find. You have to be prepared to discover anything.

A case comes to my mind about being too focused on a single target. I stopped a pickup truck with a white Hispanic male driver. It was a large Chevrolet 2500 HD 4x 4 trucks. The stop was for window tint. There was a galvanized toolbox in the truck bed positioned up next to the cab. After the stop, I walked up to the cab. I saw the entire bed of the truck was enclosed with a plastic snap on cover. The driver was very nervous and had a confusing trip plan. This led to a search of the truck. Two small bags of cocaine were found in the ashtray. The cover in the bed was pulled back. This exposed a huge homemade steel tank which encompassed three quarters of the truck bed. I lifted the toolbox cover and found it to be just the upper shell of the original item. It was used to disguise an electric pump and hoses. Wiring was traced up to the engine compartment and was found to be attached to the battery.

The driver refused to talk. We knew we had seized a large quantity of drugs. This oversized, homemade gas tank was going to be filled with drugs and we had to find the trap door. We towed the vehicle to the station and began searching it again. Discovered behind the plastic cosmetic wall covering on the back interior cab wall, we found a stack of hotel room key cards. After many hours of searching, this was all we had found. Then we realized the actual crime. He was stealing diesel fuel! The tank could hold 200 gallons. It was being filled at different fuel stations with the hotel room keys. They have a magnetic strip on the back just like a credit card. Credit card information was being stolen and placed on these cards. The driver would go to a fuel station and buy the diesel with the stolen information. He would then travel back to Miami and sell the diesel at half the cost to other truckers. We were so focused on finding drugs that we overlooked the actual criminal act. We could not see the forest through the trees.

The seed of a marijuana plant is unlike any other seed in nature. Also, marijuana stems are different as well. Look for the dried seeds or stems anywhere in the car that is visible from the outside. At night, you can utilize your flashlight to look around at the vehicles interior while standing outside. I say this because it has been an issue brought up by defense attorneys in the past. They have unsuccessfully tried to claim that since you had to use a flashlight; it was not in plain view. In Florida and in most states, it is against the law to be in possession of any part of a marijuana plant. Know the laws of your state. If any of these items are visible in the car, you now have probable cause to search the vehicle. If you suspect someone has been smoking a pipe in order to ingest drugs, you may find copper Brillo pads. Using your flashlight, you can shine the flashlight at a low angle just above the carpet. Have the beam of light sweeping across the floors. If anyone has been using the copper Brillo pads, there will be small pieces of it reflecting in your light on the carpet. This is because they will tear off pieces of the Brillo pad to stuff into the drug pipes. It is also common to use an aluminum drink can as a pipe. Examine them closely for the sides being crushed in slightly. There will be holes punched into the top for the pipe bowl and a hole underneath for the carburetor. The drinking area is used to inhale.

Another thing I watch for are burn marks in the seats. These can be simple cigarette burns which are generally more elongated in shape. When a person smokes marijuana, the seeds will heat up and often times fall out. When they hit the seat material, they will burn a perfectly round and small hole in the seat. See if the person smokes cigarettes. If they say they do not, have them explain the burn marks. Do not indicate your suspicions to them unless there is another unit with you. This will be covered in more detail later. By itself it may not be enough, but added to other discovered factors may indicate you should continue the stop.

What about the ashtray? Is it open or closed? Is there a bottle of Visine? Do you see things like a lighter? If you do, ask them if they smoke? They may say yes or no. They may answer you with a question like "cigarettes?" This tells you they have more than one thing on their mind which they could smoke. If they say no, keep these statements in mind. Why would you have a lighter in plain view if you do not smoke? Are lighters illegal? No they are not, but the items we use the most are usually laid nearby and in the open for easy access. Otherwise, they would be in the bottom of the glove box or center console.

We all know what Visine is used for. It takes the red out of your eyes. Unless you have sensitive eyes, how many people do you know carry one or more bottles of Visine with them? The sight of a bottle should also be tucked away in your mind as the list grows.

75

When you start to notice enough small indicators, suspicion builds, which could lead to you seeking, consent to search. This of course is after another officer arrives.

I refer to it as shake. Some just call it tobacco. It is simply the cigar tobacco removed from a cigar when making a "blunt." They will take a razor blade, split the cigar down the side, and remove the tobacco. Usually they put the tobacco into store bags, garbage bags, food bags, or just dump it on the floor. You will see remnants of tobacco all over the floorboards. Most of you have seen a blunt, but have you ever thought about how one is made? The internet is an incredible source for all things. As an officer, you should be visiting various web sites about drug use. Here are the instructions from one site on how to make a blunt:

Needed: Cigar, weed, knife or scissors, grinder (optional), lighter

Lick your blunt until it is moist. Take a blade and cut a straight line lengthwise from butt to tip. Stick your thumb into the opened blunt and slide the insides (known as "guts") out. Don't try to push them all out at once because you can tear the blunt up that way.

At this point you can tear or cut off the rounded end of the blunt, or leave it there. I prefer to remove it because sometimes it causes you to roll the blunt shut. In this tutorial, we'll remove the end. Using only the inner layer will cut down on the amount of nicotine.

Now that you have a nice rectangular blunt wrap, lick the edges to seal up any tears. Then, take the wrap and fold it in the center like you would for a joint.

Spread the weed evenly down the length of the blunt. (If you don't use enough weed to support the size of the wrap it will collapse in on itself while you're trying to smoke.)

Give your blunt its shape by carefully folding and rolling it up. Tuck the shorter side of the wrap around the weed, and then continue to roll it all the way. Be careful not to pinch the ends shut or roll it too tight as this will cause you to pass out from sucking too hard.

Lick the last half inch of paper lengthwise. Then, press the rest carefully down to the blunt. (Blunt type is really important here, since some blunts are stickier than others.) Do not taper the ends too much as this can cause the blunt to end up with a hole too small to pull from.

Take a lighter and run it up and down the length of the blunt while spinning it. This will dry out the moisture and give it a good bake, which makes the blunt firmer. Don't let the fire linger in one spot too long or it will burn. Bake the blunt just long enough to make it firm and a little darker in color

Hold the fire at the very tip of the blunt. Spin the blunt around to evenly distribute the flame and minimize the possibility of developing runs. (Runs can be remedied by smearing saliva on the longer side of the cherry.) (15)

Do you see the care that goes into it? Knowledge is power. How many times have you searched a car and found a razor blade. How many of us keep a razor blade in the ashtray? None of us I'm sure. They keep them to cut the side of the cigar open to make a blunt. Learn all you can about marijuana, cocaine, crack, meth, ecstasy, heroin, and stay abreast of current events. An officer who knows about criminals habits will recognize things in a vehicle or on a person that an untrained officer will not. Most of us have never been exposed to this world prior to taking the job. You do not usually get hired as a police officer if you have been a drug addict, have a criminal background, or with gang activities. Again, your agency can only teach you so much. We are hunters. As any hunter will tell you, you must be well indoctrinated to the life of your prey if you want to be successful with its capture.

Smell is the other sense which is in full swing as I approach a vehicle. Everyone knows the potent odor of marijuana. Whenever a person smokes marijuana, the odor absorbs into everything. Earlier I stated when I first walk up to a car, I ask the driver to roll up all of the windows except for the one where I am standing. What does this do? First, I can hear what is being said by the occupants without being drowned out by passing traffic. Next, because this is the only open window, all of the odors in the car are escaping out of the window past me. If anyone is or has been smoking anything in the vehicle, I will smell it. We are looking for plain view items, contraband, and residues. We smell for the trace odors of contraband. Once you have smelled the strong chemical odor of cocaine, it can be recognized coming from inside a car. That is if they have some quantity of cocaine and it has been enclosed in the car for long enough.

Generally, you can tell if something is wrong with the occupants of the vehicle by this time in the encounter. Even though we have mentioned many things, this all took place in a very short period of time. If you do not see, smell or sense anything, complete the contact so you can find the next one. If anything has drawn your attention, do not indicate this to the vehicle's occupants. I know I have already said this, but I cannot stress this enough to you. Return to your patrol car and radio for another unit. Be observant of the vehicle until your backup arrives at the scene. Tell the assisting unit what you suspect and what actions you plan to take. Coordinate the game plan together and remove the driver alone.

BEHAVIORS - 9

Police officers are generally visual people. Everyone is either visually, auditory, or emotionally oriented. We respond best to stimuli via one of these pathways. They are known as Representational System Channels. Everyone responds or learns best through the Channel that is dominate with them. The average person is about 60% visual, 30% auditory or hearing, and 10% emotional or internal feelings. Most of us comprehend a subject better when we are given visuals during an explanation. Other people are able to understand better by listening to someone or something without the visuals. Some college students discover they have to be in attendance at each class. They have to watch their professor say and illustrate everything in order to understand. If the professor just talks without the added visuals, many students will come away with the feeling they are terrible instructors. You will hear them complain; "I did not learn anything in the class." Other students can walk into a class and record the lecture. They will sit there writing notes and absorbing most of what is being said. They can listen to the tapes later and fill in many of the areas which were lost in the lecture. The visual students may take a ton of notes and never absorb any of the content. They were too busy writing and never actually listened to the lecture. Most people can only function within one Representational Channel at a time. For instance, you are talking on the phone and watching television. You can do one or the other well, but not both. One of the Channels must be turned off. You see people who are talking on the phone, but where are they looking? They will be looking down at the ground. It is a way for us to not see so we can listen. If they fail to do this, their visuals will overtake their audios. They will have to ask the person on the phone to repeat themselves.

The same understanding is applied to written statements and recordings. A written statement represents only 7% of the information that it is intended to give. For this reason alone, I hate texting. How many misunderstood messages are flying around in cyber space? With a tape recording of a person's statement, you can comprehend 45% of the intended message. You are now receiving the spoken word and tone of voice. Only a video recording will add the body language and give you 100% of the intended statement.

Police officers are taught from the beginning of their careers to watch. You always have to be watching. Our job is based on the things that we see. Is the car speeding? Did that driver run the red light? Did I see a bulge under the person's shirt? Did you see that? The person in that car, was that so and so? We are taught to look, watch, and see. Forget about the concept of look, listen, and feel. That implies too much information to comprehend. If the average person is 60% visual, 30% auditory and 10% internal feelings, think about a police officer. Our channels of communication have been altered. We are on average 87% visual, 7% auditory, 6% internal feelings. This is great! We have been taught to see things better. We are great at recognizing the big things, but we easily miss the small things. But it is the small things that are just as important as the large ones. In a study of people's behavior, before attacking someone, it is commonplace to wipe your hands on the front of your pants. You are drying them off in preparation to use them. It is wise of you to recognize this in advance. If you see someone wipe their hands on their pants roadside, does it mean you are going to be attacked? No, but the fact that you recognized it could save your life. You were paying close enough attention to see this action. Now you combine it with all of the other signals this person has shown and you have a greater chance of protecting yourself. If there were no other signs or behaviors then it could have been a simple act of drying their hands. Combined with several other things and this could indicate their fight or flight signals are going off. The stress of the encounter with you has caused their hands to sweat. How many times have you watched a video where an officer has been caught completely off guard? They will say in an interview if they are lucky enough to narrate the video, "I never saw it coming!" Never has an action been taken where the subject gave you no prior indications. We just failed to recognize them. Being able to recognize actions better than the average person makes us great for the profession we have undertaken, right? Yes and no.

We see the big picture better than most, but we have reduced our listening skills less than others. What is it which cops do all day every day? We interview people all day long. Did you know you were going that fast? Is there a reason for the speed? Tell me what happened here today. Interviews are what we do all day, but they require good listening skills. Cops can make terrible listeners. We like to be in control. We like to tell you what you saw or did. "Where are you going, to Miami?" Answer; "Yeah officer, that's right Miami." Who is in the car with you, is that your brother?" " Ah, yeah he is my brother." We have all seen and heard it before. The officer already has all of your answers ready for you.

We have to write everything down for our reports, but rarely pay close attention. Ask your friend's, especially the non-officers or your family how good of a listener you are. Usually they have just become used to the way you are or stopped trying to change you. There is a difference between listening and hearing. When you hear something it means there are sounds being made that you may recognize. When you listen, it means you understand the meaning of those sounds. Just think of it as Charlie Brown's schoolteacher. The only thing any of us ever heard was blah, blah, blah.

Here is a test to try tonight with your significant other. Ask them how their day went, but give them you're complete, and I mean complete attention. Do not lose eye contact with them. Be the most attentive person you can be. Lean forward as they talk because this shows you are interested. See how deeply it affects them. They may ask you, "What is wrong with you." "Is there something going on?" You're complete attention is strange to them. We all know someone who is a great listener. Think about why they are good listeners.

They pay attention to you. They will stop whatever they are doing and give you their time. We also know people who are terrible listeners. They constantly interrupt you or walk away while you are in mid-sentence. You will notice them looking around at other things while you are trying to talk to them. It is something you will remember about the person and can even cause you to dislike them.

To be a safe officer you have to really work at being both a good observer and listener. We all know the person who works like a machine. He writes more tickets and reports than anyone else does. Looking further, you will notice they have fewer actual arrests than anyone else. If you are stopped by them you will hear; "License, registration, and insurance. I stopped you because of this." They leave and return a moment later with your tickets that you sign and accept. They walk away and leave. You are left there thinking what a jerk that cop was to me. To the statistically oriented brass in many agencies, this officer is the best. He will receive the accolades for his high activity. If we could adjust him slightly to spend more time on the stop and ask more questions, then you would see the arrest go up. Everybody has their own cup of chowder. Everybody prefers to do different things. Some people like working DUI's while others do not. Some hate speed enforcement while others love it. Some may not like to do interdiction. But interdiction is an absolute part of every officer's job. It is involved in every aspect of patrol. Do it as safe as possible and with attention to detail. Remember, every criminal will drive at some point after nearly every crime. If the only thing you care about is tickets, then you are only doing part of your job. This may come as a blow to some people, but traffic safety can be achieved with a warning too. There are times when a driver's action requires a citation, but not always.

   We all know certain things about body language. We just don't always realize how much we know. Through our normal interactions with others while growing up, we learn to recognize things. They are never taught, but they are learned. One of the best places to see this is in the mall. Have you ever sat around and watched people walk past you? You can see the young couple in love holding hands, walking slow, stopping to window shop, and not recognizing anyone else around them. There is the couple which has been together for a while. They no longer have to give their significant other their full attention. They will start together, but then split off into different directions. They may not even notice that their other half has stopped and they are walking alone. Then there is the one who thinks he is a tuff guy and struts around with a swagger. The woman who thinks she is a runway model as she walks with one foot placed directly in front of the other causing an exaggerated hip swing. Then there is the geek who has little arm movement and walks faster than the average persons walk. Then there are the ones who are walking with confidence. They have good posture and their head is high. The one who is less confident, poor posture, and unable to look around or make eye contact. These are all small things yet they speak volumes about the person. Think back to the Seinfeld Show and how well they used different people's body language and actions to make us laugh. The reason we laughed is that we could relate to the comedy.

   Men go into a public restroom where there are urinals on the wall. If for instance there are three, side by side. You are the first guy to go into the bathroom, which one will you use. Everyone knows it will be one of the end urinals. Why is this? Because if you took the center one and another guy comes in, he will have to stand next to you. Men are uncomfortable having their privates out around other men even to go to the bathroom. This is why so many men's rooms today have newspapers on the wall for them to read as well as divider walls. It is like the window tint of the car. We get that false sense of security standing next to that small divider wall. It helps them to relax. Do our parents teach us this? No, it is just something that is learned. We also do not like to have conversations in the bathroom. The man's bathroom motto is: Go in, be quite, stay away from me, and leave.

Women have no issues going into restrooms. Unlike men who prefer to be alone, women prefer to go in platoons. How often have you heard several women at a table say "I have to go to the ladies room, would you all like to go?" Every woman at the table gets up and goes. They may not have to go to the bathroom, but their going with you anyway. They almost appear excited about it. They will go in, sit around, and talk to each other. Total strangers! How? Can you imagine the look on the face of the guys if one of them was to stand and ask if the other guys wanted to go to the bathroom with him? Self-taught behaviors.

There are many types of behavior for people. We have often seen the actions of people who get nervous or are shy. People in traffic stops who are afraid or have something to hide will often display various behaviors. Some may not be able to stand still, while others have to constantly lean against something. Some may get out of a car and start what I call the felony stretch. Their arms stretch high, arching back, and appearing to have just gotten out of bed. It is

86

the body's way of releasing stress. Others may be talkative while others will yawn. Are there any set patterns which will appear with everyone? Everyone is different and will respond to different stimuli in various ways.

A person who feels guilty and is confronted by the police will begin having increased nervous feelings. Some are able to hide these feelings pretty well while others cannot. They will not all be apparent, but they all will be visible if you are watching for them. Once you are confident something is wrong, it is time to go after the person's internal feeling. This is the third of the three representational channels. It is the stimulus applied to expose their feelings. They are the physical and psychological reactions to stress. You use this by adding stimulus to a person so you can observe their behavior. This is known as kinesics. Communications are expressed through body language, tone of voice, and spoken words. It will be the same as we discussed earlier with written statements. The amount of information we receive from someone through spoken words is only 7%. You can change the meaning of the spoken words with tone of voice which accounts for another 38% of information. Generally, a person's volume and pitch increases with stress. Anger can increase the speed. We have all seen angry people talk and it is rarely slow and deliberate. A person's body language provides us with 55% of the information we are to receive.

We are watching for the information to spill from a person in clusters. A single action may not indicate deception. When you notice a person's heart rate increase, skin blush, and their eyes dart around, this can be indicative of stress. The cluster of things says something is wrong. Watching a person's eyes can tell you things about what they are saying.

Most people when asked a question can tell you the truth without thought. When the information has to be removed from an internal file, aka memory, they will generally move their eyes high and to the left. This is not true for the entire population, but it is similar to assuming everyone is right handed. The chances are they will be except for about 10% who will be lefties. For this generalization of eye assessment, we will play the odds. You would have to ask a person numerous base line questions of known facts to determine how a person retrieves the information. You can gather much of the information from their pedigree questions. Now you have their basic known information, you can have them expound on the facts. If with these base questions they move their eyes high left, then they are seeking the information, as would most people. If you asked for a person's family birth dates, they may have to think about it. You will see them look high and left as they "look" at the numbers. They may initially go high right and then go to the left. That is ok because they are trying to find the file that the information is stored within. Now as you ask someone questions and they vary their eye movements drastically, the chances are they are being creative. It may not mean they are lying to you, but maybe they are not telling the whole truth. If it is current events such as where are you coming from or where are you going, little to no thought should be necessary. Very little eye movement should take place. Little if any hesitation should occur. It is not much different than asking someone their name. They should be able to easily tell you.

Always keep in mind that there are cultural differences. Eye movements is an involuntary action that can work based on your observations of their eyes with simple questions. There are cultures where people do not make good eye contact. They look down all of the time, especially when speaking to a police officer or other authority figure. Many people who have recently arrived in the U.S. from Central or South America will be very passive and none confrontational with authority. Many who come from countries that are controlled by oppressive governments see all authority the same. Keep these issues in mind when watching the eyes.

When you are talking to someone and you ask a question that should stir an emotional response, they should look down. Something that is very close or harmful to them will cause them to look down and to the right. With the eyes down, this is an emotional response. If you are interviewing someone and they begin to look down, you will need to mirror them. Stay on an emotional line of questioning. By this I mean with questions and statements like "I can only imagine how you feel" "What are you feeling right now?" or "How do you think that makes them feel?" It is also a good time to move into their personal zone. Move within 3 feet of them if you feel it is safe. They are in their internal emotion channel.

For a more comprehensive study on the subject, every police officer should take as many kinesics courses as possible. They should even re-take classes they have had in the past to refresh their knowledge. Dealing with people is our job. Understanding body language is critical to us in performing our job safely.

When asking someone a yes or no question, the only acceptable answer is a yes or no answer. When a simple direct question is asked of a person, they should be able to answer it simply and directly. When they start hesitating or repeating the question back to you, they are trying to buy time to figure out the best answer. It may be the truth, but they had to decide whether to give it to you.

Once the stop has taken place, you become suspicious of the occupants. You call for another unit to back you up. There is a driver and right front seat passenger. The backup unit arrives and you explain to your partner your suspicions. Explain what it is you are going to do and what you want from them. Not everyone is going to have the same experience and you do want to have to explain everything in the middle of something going wrong. Be sure to use good approach and cover techniques. Do not walk up to the same side of the car side by side. You are presenting yourselves as easy multiple targets to the occupants inside. The cover officer can stay at the rear of the vehicle or to the outside of the approaching officer. No matter the number of occupants in the car, whether or not you have the driver exit, the approaching officer has cover from the other officer. If you have the driver exit the car, the rear cover officer can watch and direct the driver out of the car. The approach officer watches the passengers in the car. You remove the driver, pat him down, and move to the passenger's side of your car. From here, you have the drivers back turned to his car and you are facing it. This serves several functions. First, the driver and the passengers cannot communicate with one another. Second, it places the driver between you and the car. You can see if anything is happening past the driver. The cover officer should be continuing their observation of the car. If someone starts to get out of the car, you can both react quickly.

This is a good place to talk about video cameras. A video camera has its pro's and con's. All too often, I see officers playing everything up for the camera. They know it is there and recording everything. Often times, they will not act naturally because they know the camera is on. This distraction can also interfere with what you are trying to accomplish with the subjects in the car. You no longer have complete concentration on the situation. So often, I see officers who have the violator place their hands on the hood of their car to be patted down and handcuffed. It is an all right method to use, but they are doing it from the front of their own car. They are doing it for the sake of the camera. They have their backs turned to the violator's car which creates additional dangers to them. A passenger in the violator's car can come out before you have time to react. We have all seen it happen on video. What would happen if their patrol car is struck from behind? Both the officer and the violator will be killed or seriously injured.

You approach the passenger's side and ask the driver to exit the car and bring the keys. This prevents the passenger from sliding over and driving away. It also makes it harder for the driver to re-enter the car to leave. One of the first things I will do is ask if I can pat them down for weapons. They are now outside the car and on a level playing field with you. It is the time to clear them of any weapons they may have. I will remove any weapons including pocketknives and cell phones from them. What did you say? A cell phone can be used as a weapon. It can be used to conceal a weapon and contraband. I have seen people wearing several cell phones. Be sure check the battery area and the inside of the phone if they are wearing one that does not work. With the battery out, it can hold a small amount of contraband. But more importantly, do not let people talk on their cell phones while you are with them. They could easily call someone else to tell them where they are and what is happening with them. If the violator intends you harm, they could have their own backup arrive in moments.

I know some officers will teach and swear by the method of having the drivers always exit their car. It is in my opinion a bad idea. It places them on equal ground to you. You always want the upper hand. When the subjects are out on foot and they draw a weapon, they will have the same options as you. They can attempt their actions at their own discretion. There is a reason why more officers are assaulted while attempting to arrest someone. It is because they are for that moment your equal. If you traded places with the bad guy and said in your mind you had to take this officer out, when would you do it? You would initiate your assault when you were out of the car. This is when the officer is closest and most vulnerable to you. We have seen and heard about it forever. Inmates in prison are constantly practicing various techniques to overcome you as you arrest them. They can advance on you, take cover from you, or attack you and run. We learned earlier that if they had a weapon, we would need more than 30 feet to protect ourselves by using a weapon from our utility belt. How close is the average person to you at a traffic stop? Usually just outside of our personal space of 2-3 feet.

If they are restricted to the confines of the car, their options are limited. If they start to exit their car, you will give them the verbal commands to stop and re-enter the car. If you have to tell them more than once you should see the danger flags. As we will soon see, if you have to repeat your commands, their minds are preoccupied. This person could be dangerous. You had better start doing something which could include drawing your weapon. See what their response is now. Are they still not listening to your commands? You had better be calling for backup. Are they unarmed from what you can see, but not advancing yet still not listening to you? Keep your distance, maintain cover, and wait for the backup. Are they advancing on you? What secondary weaponry are you trained with and have available. What is their physical size compared to you? There are many factors to consider in a split second. Just remember, despite what some people believe you are not paid to get injured or killed. You take the immediate action required to stop the threat.

Another study from Force Science News, Transmission # 155, involves what some are calling The Fatigue Threshold. Remember when I said that it was good to know various fighting techniques, but the best defense to a fight is in avoiding one. All fights eventually end on the ground. This is why so many agencies are now practicing ground fighting techniques. Break away and separate as fast as possible in a fight. Here is what this study tells us about an all-out fight for your life. "Certain muscles can be affected after approximately 30 seconds of maximum-intensity exercise. While "roughly" 1 to 5 minutes might seem a likely "normal" range, don't figure on most people being able to hold out for more than 2 minutes or so. You don't have much time to get a suspect under control before you're going to be in trouble. The suspect may not tire as quickly as you because it's a lot easier to resist than to overcome resistance. The exact point can be influenced not only by the officer's fitness level but also by such factors as the intensity of the altercation, the number of suspects and officers involved, the suspect's physical condition, environmental influences (heat, humidity, cold), the officer's equipment (20-lb. belt, motion-restricting ballistic vest, heat-retaining wool uniform) and the combatants' will to overcome and survive. Your recovery may take as long as a quarter-hour. Once an officer hits the wall, all gains are lost all advantages evaporate. The reasonable officer understands that any suspect who is willing to fight the police with such intensity that he can bring the officer to the limits of his strength is dangerous and cannot be allowed to control the outcome. In most cases you can tell when you are about to reach your physical limit, although you may still be surprised at how rapidly you can fade, especially where upper-body strength is concerned. When you sense you're nearing your threshold, you must act quickly and decisively to control the suspect." (16)

From the car, the only time they have to assault you with a firearm is in your approach. Again, if you will follow the rules as we have discussed, you will still have many advantages. We know how to physically approach the car; our disadvantage is almost always going to be in our mental planning. Is your head in the right place to deal with this problem now? When you are at home, you leave the stress of the job at the job. When you are at work, you leave the stress of your personal life at home. Never should the two intermingle for very long. I know you cannot just turn off a switch. If you cannot concentrate on what you are doing, especially when interacting with someone, you should take a day off.

An example of keeping someone in the car is an event that occurred in Louisiana involving the traffic stop of a van occupied by two males. As it was reported in the news is the following:

The trooper exited his vehicle and asked the driver to do the same. As the driver stepped out of his vehicle, he immediately turned towards the trooper and began firing several shots at the trooper with a handgun. As the trooper took cover behind his patrol car, twice bullets from the driver's gun struck him. They then fled the scene westbound on Interstate 20. (17)

There is the case of the Texas Trooper who stops the pickup truck. He suspects the driver of DUI. The driver has made him nervous enough where several times he has grabbed the handle of his service weapon and blades his weapon away from the driver. I believe he plays up many things for the camera. He turns his back on the occupants to bring a bottle of liquor to set on his hood after having the driver exit the vehicle. The driver is wearing a long trench coat and there is a passenger in the truck. He has to repeat his commands several times to the driver. He decides to arrest the driver for DUI next to the truck and the passenger. The passenger exits, distracts him, and they each pull guns firing over 20 rounds at the trooper. Only by the grace of God did he survive. It is easy to be a Monday morning armchair quarterback. All that I want to stress is with a few simple changes to our strategy, I know we can not only survive more encounters, but prevent them as well. We all watch these events unfold and say I would never do it that way. But I know we all have many times over. We just have to try harder not to do them again.

Now you are separating the occupants. Even if there is only the driver in the car with no passengers, you will ask them to exit the car. Tell them to bring the keys after another unit is with you. If you have enough suspicions about the driver, which causes you to have him, exit the car, then you will want another unit with you. If there was nothing about the stop that created your increasing interest, then they should have stayed in the car. You should release them as soon as you complete your enforcement actions.

The purpose of separating the driver from the passengers is because you suspected they were up to something wrong. If they are not, when questioned with a few basic questions, their answers will be identical. However, if they are up to no good, there will be discrepancies. Two people traveling around together can easily tell you about the events which started their time together to the present. There are people who have done nothing wrong at the moment, but feel compelled to lie to you. It is hard to put together a lie and have several people explain it the same way. Because it is not tucked away in their memory file, they have to try to remember what they did. They can even practice their story, which they never do, and still not get it right. If you direct enough various questions toward them, it will fall apart.

Can you lie to them if you suspect them of wrongdoing? The answer is yes. They are easily played against one another because they are criminals together. They know they can never fully trust one another. Those long pauses they presented are causing stress. The brain takes more time to create a lie than it does to tell the truth. The statements a person makes have to match their body language. People like to talk with their hands, but there are times when a guilty person may not. A point they try to stress appears wrong. You will recognize it if you are paying attention.

Stress causes confusion and confusion causes stress. This stress will cause change and the change initiates the leaking of clusters. I have watched a man who became so nervous he fainted roadside. The stress just reached a point that his brain said "that's enough let's say good night." Another time I watched as a guy was talking to us roadside and chewing gum. He became so nervous that he quit producing saliva and the gum started to stick all over his lips. The first guy had a small bag of cocaine and a little weed. The second guy had 500 pounds of marijuana.

Another clue to a person's behavior is in their listening abilities. Once the stress increases, a condition known as audio occlusion kicks in. They will no longer hear or understand you. They are on a mission in their mind. Be very careful if you are presented with this person. Often times they will do no more than mumble, but not while they are looking at you. They are trying to determine their best options and are stressed out. If you have ever been in a high stress event, you may not remember any sounds. Your body is in overdrive to save itself.

I spent a lot of time examining the video tapes of police officers who were assaulted and sometimes murdered. At the time, I was teaching police departments around the country a course in highway interdiction techniques. My goal then, as it is now, was officer safety. I wanted to see if I could find any verbal or physical actions of people before they attacked. It did not take long before I realized I had. I do not know if I am the only one to recognize it, but I do know I have tried to teach it to as many officers as will listen. You can look back at almost any video of an officer being assaulted and there was always one common denominator. The officer had to repeat their commands to the subject several times just before the attack took place. I do not care how old a video is, it still teaches us a lesson. I have shown videos of officers and been asked if I had something newer. We have been killed the same way since the beginning of law enforcement. It does not matter what was used or when they died. What does matter is the how it occurred. Watch all of the videos, regardless of their age and you can learn something that may save you later.

There is the video of a Texas constable who conducts a traffic stop. Three subjects who will later assault and kill him occupy the car. We watch as he gets the driver out car and back by the trunk of their car. He returns to the driver's window and begins to talk to the subjects inside. You can watch the driver stretch. It is the felony stretch. The officer asks about the trunk and the front right passenger exits. The constable tells him to "stay in the car, I'll get it." He repeats himself several more times before not saying it again. The passenger was already on a mission. The passenger knew there was marijuana in the trunk and they were not going to be arrested. Many people have mentioned that the passenger also takes his hat off as he gets out of the car. It is a good observation. Explain why you would wear a hat in the car and take it off when you exit. Some even say it would be normal to take off your hat before a fight. Once they are standing at the rear of the car the constable is standing at the trunk. The driver is behind him and the right front passenger is to his right. The constable is asking whose bag is whose and the passenger just quits listening. He mumbles a couple times and even the constable does not understand him. His mind is preoccupied as he instructs the driver in Spanish to get the officer. The constable was killed with his own gun. The constable had to repeat himself so many times, but he never sees this as a danger to himself. He never asks for back up. I do not know this for sure, but I question if many of his actions were performed for the camera. He had to know what was in the trunk, yet he kept pushing them. They snapped and he paid the ultimate sacrifice.

There is the video of the female officer in Texas who smells marijuana in the car and the driver is on probation. She instructs him out of the car and tells him to put his hands on the hood of her car. She has to keep repeating herself as he turns and punches her. He beats her into a coma roadside and unsuccessfully tries to remove her handgun.

There is also the video of the Georgia deputy who stops a subject believed to be involved in an armed robbery. The car stops and the driver exits. The deputy asked him for his license as the subject reaches into the car. The deputy tries repeatedly to verbally stop him as he moved closer. The subject comes around with a gun and kills him. As with the other videos, the officers repeated their commands and did what most cops do. When you do not listen to me, I am going to get closer to you. When you recognize they are not listening to you create distance and wait. Just like earlier when we spoke about Representational Channels, when their mental or internal feelings are on full speed ahead, their visuals, and audios will be turned off. Only one Channel will play at a time.

Watch other videos as the officer's actions repeat themselves. They will reiterate their commands to the subjects who will ignore them. The officers fail to wait on back up and the officers get closer instead of backing away. Remember our shooting ally known as distance? We have to maintain our distance. When you are commanding someone to do something and they are moving to an area you cannot see, back away. Do not be afraid to draw your weapon if you need to. Take the offensive by becoming defensive and live. Television has gotten many officers killed. You see the person you are dealing with has a gun, and you yell "drop the gun!" Your action should have been sight picture, sight alignment, breath, trigger squeeze. This is stated as an example only, but your actions had better be swift. Do not forget your instinctive shooting techniques. You do not wait for them to shoot first. You do not give them any additional advantages to kill you. If they have a weapon and you hesitate, the outcome may be fatal to you.

I will describe an event that occurred and finished on a positive note. A trooper is parked watching traffic. A pickup truck speeds by. The driver, upon seeing the trooper, brakes and actually turns around in his seat to watch what the trooper will do. The driver's window is half way down. The trooper sees the unusual reaction of the driver (remember these behavioral reactions from earlier as they realize they see the police) and attempts a traffic stop for unlawful speed. The driver of the vehicle travels a short distance before they begin to slow down. They move to the outside shoulder and travel slowly about one half mile before stopping. This can be a significant event. You have to have red flags going up in your mind. Why would someone not immediately stop for the police? The windows are tinted and it is unknown how many occupants there are in the vehicle. What was the driver doing inside the vehicle while it traveled slowly down the shoulder? The trooper maintains a lot of distance between his vehicle and their car while they were driving slowly. The driver could stop suddenly and exit which puts you in a bad position. The trooper has removed his seatbelt and has called in his location. A backup unit is already enroute to him. The vehicle finally stops. The trooper positions his unit almost three cars length back and completely off the road at an angle. The trooper opens his door and steps out, but stays behind his opened door. He has also already drawn his service weapon and holds it down to his side. The driver still has the window partially down. The driver of the vehicle keeps looking back at the trooper through his side view mirror. The trooper sees that the brake lights are still on and he does not attempt to walk up to the car. The trooper stays in his position of cover and sees his backup approaching. The trooper calls for the driver to exit the vehicle, but the driver does not comply. The trooper calls repeatedly for the driver to exit, but he still fails to comply. The driver eventually puts the car into park and exits the vehicle. The trooper brings his gun up and orders the driver to the ground. Now the driver complies with the orders. The backup unit has arrived and he deploys a shotgun. The passenger is removed from the vehicle. Both are handcuffed and secured.

Remember that not all situations are the same. This quit being just another traffic stop when the driver of the vehicle began to act suspiciously. The trooper called for another unit to be enroute to his location early. The driver failed to obey commands and the trooper had to repeat himself. He had already positioned himself some distance back and behind cover. His gun was pulled and at a low ready position. What were their reasons for this erratic behavior? There were drugs, warrants for the driver's arrest, and a gun.

Do you see the deadly mistakes made in the earlier cases as compared to the last one? There was the officer's failure to wait for backup before proceeding with a confrontation. Once danger should have been recognized, there was a hesitation to react properly and with enough force to control the situation. When you suspect criminal activity, do not let suspects know what you are thinking. I even like to cut it off short if I know something is wrong. Tell them you will be right back, I am only going to write you a warning and send you on your way. Another will be "You will be on your way in a moment." I know the tactic works because after they are arrested or detained, they are placed into the rear of a patrol car. They are recorded and on the tape recordings, you will hear them telling each other. "Why didn't you do this or that?" The driver will say "you heard him; he was going to let us go." You can even see their behaviors go from tense and nervous to a more relaxed state. This topic will be touched on in the next chapter. The one that makes me cringe is when there is single officer at a traffic stop and they smell marijuana inside the car. The officer will say, "Do I smell marijuana in your car?" or "Is that marijuana I smell?" or "I smell something in your car. What is it?" I know we think of most potheads as easygoing stoners, but the fact of the matter is they kill many of us every year. Almost all criminals smoke pot. Smoking pot in most states is a crime. What do they care if they are caught with a little pot. Never let them know what you know. Keep the advantage over them at all times. You do not know what this person has done prior to your encounter.

Everyone has little things that work for them. When you have the opportunity to work with different agencies, try to go along. Watch how they work and try to find methods that they employ. You will find that many of these can be incorporated into your own tactics. I have patrolled with the United States Border Patrol in El Paso and worked many checkpoints with them in Texas and New

Mexico. I patrolled with the Texas DPS in the Valley for several weeks. I rode along with the Mississippi Highway Patrol. I have watched and learned from everyone. I was on I-10 one night at the Sierra Blanca checkpoint east of El Paso watching the Border Patrol at work. As cars drive up, the agent will either wave them through or over to a secondary inspection. Agents have their own behaviors, car types, and other things that interest them. Some say the people just look out of the ordinary. When you stand there all day, watching cars slow and drive by, you get a feeling for ordinary. Some are too friendly, too talkative, too tense, or just look afraid. I cannot tell you exactly what to look for because everyone is different. What is important is to start paying attention to your own stops and the stops of others. Learn to slow things down and watch for unusual behaviors. They will stand out like a beacon. You will see them and start developing your own set of criminal behaviors that work best for you.

Behaviors are applied to the identification of terrorist as well. I had a former Israeli intelligence officer tell me even though a terrorist is on jihad; it is still not a simple task for them to commit suicidal homicide. They could usually see a terrorist in public because of his behavior. He may think he's going to heaven with a bunch of virgins, but their handlers always have to give them barbiturates to help calm them down before the journey. They would sweat profusely and not respond to verbal commands. They are on a mission with a lot on their mind. Sound familiar? Their mind is on a set task. This person is dangerous. They are operating in their internal Channel.

The FBI, stated in the September 2005 Law Enforcement

Bulletin;

"Patrol officers need to know, for example, that suicide bombers may wear clothing out of sync with the weather, their location, or their social positions; carry heavy luggage, bags, or backpacks; repeatedly and nervously pat their upper bodies with their hands; display hyper-vigilant stares; or fail to respond to voice commands." (18)

It all sounds familiar because the behaviors of the criminal will be the same as the terrorist. They are both filled with nervous feelings. Someone walking with a gun on the street will repeatedly check that it is secure by touching it. They may check with their hands or with their arms, but their actions will be noticeable.
I was assigned to our Dignitary Protection Detail for several years. We were trained in advance preparations and security measures of the protectee. In our case, it was the Lieutenant Governor of Florida. He was the Lt. Governor under Jeb Bush, the president's brother. It was post 9-11 and we worked hard to cover the basics with the manpower, which was available. In our training sessions, we were always taught to watch for people behaving differently and watch the hands. When you are working a crowd line, you are always watching the hands that are being presented. Some of us would be watching ahead to where we were walking. Others are working the back of the crowd. Still others would be behind the protectee watching the behaviors and facial expressions of the people in the crowd. But you were always looking for the person who appeared different. Maybe it was with their smile. Bad guys know we are looking for their behavioral changes. Everyone there is smiling except one guy. Maybe that guy smiles, but you can see it is a fake smile. Look at

104

yourself in a mirror and see how many muscles are moved in your face when you actually smile. Then fake a smile and see how many fewer muscles are used. They will usually give themselves away. It was a great experience and I learned a lot about people's behaviors.

I can never stress to you just how important this last chapter has been to me and should be to you. We need to constantly practice and watch people's behaviors. We need to listen closely to the words they speak. We need to pay very close attention to the behaviors of people in order to determine what is normal and what is dangerous. Practice and training in the area of body language interpretations can give you the skills, which may allow you to recognize danger seconds before it happens. These seconds are exactly what we need to act before having to react to a situation.

THE CULMINATION OF TACTICS -10

There are many types of questions that we need to be asking. If the violator can answer our questions in a way, which satisfies your curiosity, good keep moving. There's nothing to see here. If not, keep asking questions until they can satisfy you. If they cannot satisfy you then it is time to find out why. I have had people complain over the years because I asked if they had ever been arrested or was on probation. There is nothing wrong with this question. The information of a person's arrest record can be critical to your safety. How many of your best friends and family have an extensive arrest record. The number will be low because we will not associate with them. Criminals have criminals as friends and associates. Only 3% of offenders interviewed for and by the FBI in regards to attacks on officers stated, they had no prior criminal history. This was only from a random group of 50 violators. (19) Therefore, 97% of the random group did have prior arrest. Do you understand its importance now? They should be asked the question near the beginning of an encounter.

Why am I asking them so many questions? The answer is easy, because I want too. There is no limit on what you ask as long as the encounter remains consensual. If I feel there is a need for it, I will ask as many questions as I can. It is my job. We are supposed to be inquisitive.

No single answer from a subject will give you everything you need, but it will lead to more questions. Where are you going? Where are you coming from? These two questions start to establish the bases for the remainder of the stop. If they say from work, then ask what kind of work? After they answer you, ask yourself if their appearance matches their stated work? They do not appear to have any nervous behaviors and they can easily present all of their documents. Take the appropriate actions for the violation and move on. Often I watch as officers spend entirely too much time with simple stops. Do not try to make something out of nothing. Do not let your drive cause you to waste time. Find and stop the next violation.

You ask the same questions to someone else and they say they are traveling from Houston, Texas to Tampa, Florida. You already see they have a Florida driver's license and they are by themselves. Their address is in Tampa and you can see no luggage in the passenger's compartment. The registration shows a third party owns the car. Is there enough information to ask for consent already? Yes and no. More information is needed to establish a higher probability of criminal activity. Consent can be asked of anyone at any time. There is no need to waste everyone's time if there are no substantiating facts. It goes back to trying too hard to make something out of nothing. How does this person look? Have they been sleeping in the car? How well kept and rested do they appear? Are there fast food bags and caffeine items visible? Was this trip for business or pleasure? You ask them, "When did you travel there and when did you leave to return?" These are all viable questions in order to obtain additional information. How well can they answer these questions? Does the line of questioning create additional nervous reactions? Can you see them becoming more nervous or starting to get angry? Sometimes they will ask you questions. "Why are you asking me these questions?" I have heard this response more than once. The tension they are experiencing is causing them stress. Remember, stress causes confusion and confusion cause stress. They may start asking you questions in an effort to delay or divert you. Stay on task and in control. Another spontaneous statement you will hear is; "Do you want to search my car? Go ahead I don't have anything in there." But while they are saying this they are unable to stand still. What their body language is telling you is, "I hope you do not search the car because I am so friendly and co-operative." Often times they are looking everywhere or staring at the car. People still believe that if they tell you all is ok, you should believe them. When they offer you this opportunity, take it. Ask them, "Is it ok if I search your car?"

Based on the circumstances which you are confronted with,

there are many things you can ask. They just need to be relevant with
the information you received which caused you to start asking the
questions. If there is more than one person in the car, be sure to
separate them before asking questions. Before you separate them, be
sure to have backup. I will repeat this again because it is so
important, but do a pat down for weapons.

Ask them; what is your name? What is the name of the other
person in the car with you? What time did you start out together?
What is the exact location you are traveling to today? How many
times have you stopped someone on a trip and they do not know
where they are going? When you ask them, how are you going to get
there? They will tell you that they are going to call someone when
they get close. Ask them for the number they are supposed to call.
Ask them from where are they to call? What exit are you supposed to
take? If they are not related ask them how are they dividing the cost
of the trip? Did they stay anywhere along the way? If yes, then
where? When did you last eat and where? Simple questions any two
people can answer if they are on a trip together. The problem will
exist when they are not sure about what the other one is answering.
Lie to them if you think they are lying to you. When they give you
an answer ask them, "Why would the other person tell me this or
that?" For example, the passenger tells you that they are going to
Miami. You ask him if they are supposed to stop anywhere else.
They will answer "not that I am aware of." Then you ask why would
the driver say you are going somewhere else if you say you are not?
This really puts the pressure on them. When they are real nervous a
great question to ask is, "Why would someone call the police today
to say you have drugs in your car?" Now just think about the

question a moment. You are a drug smuggler and a police officer asked you that question. In your mind you are thinking who would have snitched on me. Now you know the body language would be pouring out in clusters at this point.

You have to look at the answers people give you and see if they make sense. Would you possibly do anything this person did? If not, you need to keep digging. In the end, things may still not make any sense to you. However, at least you can say you exhausted all of your options to figure out why. Some people have never made sense at anything they have ever done. You have to accept it and move on. Incredibly there are still many judges in the system who cannot believe the evil people do. I recently had a judge explain in court he finds it hard to believe that anyone who has ever been in the system would give the police consent to search. Verbal consents have always sufficed for consent in the jurisdiction which I work. Whenever I ask for consent, I will make sure my partner is present to witness the consent.

When asking someone if you can search their car, ask them if you can search their car. Yes, I did repeat myself. This may sound strange, but there are many officers who ask if we can look in your car. In many areas this means that you can stand on the outside and look inside. We want to search your car and all of the contents in the car. Another good question at this point is to ask if there is anything in the vehicle that does not belong to you. Give them a chance to distance themselves from anything illegal. One other good question is to ask if there is anything illegal in the car. You or I can instantly answer the question; they will have to think about it. Another standard answer to the question is, "not that I know of."

110

There is always new case law arriving from the courts overseeing the rules for your jurisdiction. Follow those rules closely. Do not allow a good case to fall to the wayside over a small misstep on your part. It will happen inevitably, but try to cross all of your T's and dot your I's. In some areas, it is required that you get consent to search form signed. In other areas, it is ok to ask for everything verbally. Do what your prosecutors and department want you to do. I also have a K-9 present with me all of the time. His nose and the free air sniff on the exterior of the car is my probable cause. A K-9 alert in Florida is probable cause to search the vehicle. I know in other areas of the country it is not.

I encourage everyone to read about the drug trade. Where and how are drugs manufactured? How are they coming into the areas you work? With this small amount of information, you can interdict drugs. Not just the street level nickel bag people, but smugglers. Make contact with the local narcotics investigators and DEA. Talk to them and let them know what you are trying to do. Let them know you will give them any information on any arrest you make. You will be surprised how many cases will tie into many of their cases. Ask them what kind of cases they are currently working and how are they moving the drugs into the area? Where do they think the drugs are coming from? Look at a map and find the most direct roadway that leads to your area. Ask them about the couriers they have seen and if there is any intelligence, they could give to you to watch for. Do they recognize any trends? Are the mules normally single or double males? Maybe they like to use females. If so, are they usually traveling alone? Do they use counter surveillance techniques like chase cars?

Currently there are many trends in the drug business. They are not surprising trends either. Some are frightening. They were all received from the DEA current trends information on their website. For instance, most of the MDMA, which enters the country, arrives from Canada. Overall, there really has not been a change in the use of MDMA. It is neither higher nor lower in consumption. The manufacturers of the substance in Canada have decided to try and change that. How is the shocking part. They are spiking the MDMA tablets with methamphetamine. This is much more addictive and will cause all of the party crowds to become very addicted, very fast.

The Mexican DTO's (Drug Trafficking Organizations) are having some success in the transportation and distribution of Heroin into the northeast. No other region of the country has a heroin problem as large as this region. Why not make it worse! The Mexican heroin production is not only up, but it is producing white heroin. Mexican heroin has traditionally been brown or black tar.

Shipments of ephedrine and pseudo ephedrine are easily diverted from the ports of Mexico. They are not controlled as they are here in the U.S. What this means is an increase in meth production in Mexico and transportation into the U.S. The greatest drug threat across the nation is still cocaine. It is followed by methamphetamine. (20)

If you make an arrest or have probable cause to detain people, you place them into the rear of your patrol car. This is where one of our greatest tools exists. The concealed audio recorder and microphone system. You have to find out what is allowed in your state, but in Florida, no one has any rights to an expectation of privacy while in a patrol car. We will often place covert microphones in the rear passenger compartments of our vehicles. There are as many people in prison from their taped patrol car statements as most other investigative tools. They talk about the drugs, where it is, and who put it there when they were pulled over. They tell us if there are hidden guns and numerous times, we have had to take female defendants to the hospital because it was discovered they had placed drugs inside a body cavity.

In the 1970's and 1980's, almost all of the drugs entering the United States came into South Florida. It had become the second home to nearly every South American drug lord. It was a financial Mecca. Drugs left through Florida and money returned. This is where I started in the interdiction business.

No one in the 1970's and few in the early 1980's were involved with interdiction. The State of Florida tasked the FHP with creating a K-9 corps to combat the drugs as they left Miami. President Reagan had sent Vice President George Bush to south Florida to lead the war on drugs. In July 1984, I was asked to assist a K-9 trooper with his interdiction duties. It was to be a pilot program to determine how effective we could be as a team. It turned out to be very effective. Few if any officers in the country were working full time interdiction. We had no one to train us because there was no one involved in interdiction. We read the news and were aware that Miami was home to all of the drug trafficking organizations. We took out a map and said if we were going to transport drugs from Miami, what route would we take? Of those routes, which ones seemed to encompass our area of patrol? That location was where we went to look for drug smugglers. We started out only working late at night. We learned over time it did not matter what time of day you worked. The drugs were going to travel day and night. We learned on our own what people liked, what the transportation trends were, and more importantly how quickly they would change. They will use a method of transportation until it is no longer effective. The cartels have an expectation of loss to law enforcement. The majority of the product will get through. If this method worked that month, but then started to be discovered by law enforcement, then the method would be changed.

The smugglers rarely attempted to hide anything. We would stop cars with hundreds of pounds of marijuana in the back seat. We seized over 900 pounds of cocaine from the bed of a pickup truck and over 700 pounds of cocaine sitting in the passenger compartment of a van. Over the years, as more and more law enforcement people became involved, their tactics started to change. Because of the heavy police presence in South Florida and the Caribbean, the Columbian cartels started to move their product through Mexico. They arranged for Mexico and some of its early cartels to transport the drugs over the border. It is still flowing across the border today. The country of Mexico is for the most part a narco state. The drug trade supports the bulk of its economy. Mexico has always suffered with its ruling class. You are either in the upper class or the lower class. There is nothing in between. No middle class. Anyone who has ever worked in any facet of government will tell you Mexico is very corrupt. A few have everything while most have nothing. Economics is the driving force of everything. I once had a high ranking member with the National Security Advisors Office tell me the reason why we do not close down our border with Mexico is because of socio-economics.' If we were to shut the border down tight, the economy of Mexico would collapse. The massive rush to the United States would be overwhelming. Can we stop the illegal drug flow into the U.S.? Yes, we can, but we choose not to. The State Department is far more important than the Justice Department. Drugs still arrive into south Florida, but with nowhere near the volume it had in the 1980's.

If you stop someone and they tell you they are coming from a source area, it is a good start. Check out the rest of the story and see if it makes sense. Does the interior of the car match the trip plan in regards to visible items? Do not be placed into a false sense of security when it comes to families. My partner and I stopped a van once with luggage on the roof. The driver said he was going to his cousin's house. The female passenger stated the driver was her husband and they were taking their three children to Disney World. The driver was asked what the cousin's address was. He did not know the address, but he was to call him when he got to the exit. We said give us the number and we will call to get the address for you. Then the story changed again. He said he lost the number, but he knew how to get there. Ok, we said how do you get there. He stared down the road at the large golden arches sign and said, "I am supposed to turn at the McDonalds." The location of the stop was 20 miles south of the interstate to go to Orlando. The female passenger said they were going to Disney World and did not know anything about the visit to the cousin's house. The driver described the passenger as his girlfriend. We asked him why she thinks she is married to him and he thought a moment and said, "Because we have been together a long time." There was something about the vehicle that did not make sense. We ran the K-9 around the van. The dog would move away from the vehicle and then track back. It was a

115

definite change in behavior, but different. Then it hit us. Why would you travel in a van, even with three children, and put your luggage out in the weather. There was more than enough room in the rear of the van to hold the luggage. Inside of the luggage on the roof was over 300 pounds of marijuana. The woman had been paid to travel with the driver. When the trip was over to deliver the drugs, he would take her and the children to Disney World. It was a rental family added to the load vehicle to try to give legitimacy to the appearance. The driver could not control his behaviors as he approached and passed us. The K-9 was detecting the odor of marijuana, which, due to the wind, was passing over the van. He was wind scenting away from the van and then trying to follow the odor back to the van. Due to the height of the vehicle and the cross winds, there was a void area of odor when you got close to the side of the van.

I will give you another case scenario to bring everything together. We stopped a guy in a pickup truck. He is traveling alone. He says he is going home to Gainesville, Florida, from Key West. He states he had gone on vacation for a few days and his girlfriend stayed at home because he was going to go SCUBA diving. All of his equipment was in the back of the truck. What do we have so far? He is nervous, but this could be just because he was pulled over by the police. He has gone on vacation alone for a few days even though he has a girlfriend. Still this could be plausible, except that it will take you 10-12 hours to drive there one way. There is one-day travel in each direction. He only went down for a couple of days. He points out his equipment is in the back of the truck. I look and see fins, mask, snorkel, and an old air tank. I do not see any other equipment.

Being a SCUBA diver myself I know what he has is equipment to go snorkeling. There is not a regulator or bouncy compensator. Guess where the drugs are? That's right; it was in the air tank. When you pulled the plastic boot off of the bottom of the tank, there was actually a screwed down plate. He had 10 pounds of marijuana.

The strategy behind interdiction is simple. Take your time and be observant. Be cautious and stay with it when you are suspicious. Do not be fooled by the presence of families or women. Women are actually very much preferred in smuggling because the DTO's think we are less likely to stop females. Ask the questions to see if the answers match their behaviors and the appearance of the vehicle. Does everything look the way it should based upon the statements they have made to you.

Another topic, which is very prevalent today, is human trafficking. Most of us never realize to what degree this is taking place around the country. Many of the same DTO's around the world are involved in the human trade as well. It can be just as lucrative financially, yet it does not carry the same stiff penalties as being caught with drugs. Most police officers, if they were to stop a human smuggling vehicle would never know it. There are differences with the people and the vehicle that can give them away. Just as before with drugs and other crimes, a police officer who takes their time will notice the differences. You have to be paying attention.

All of the human traffickers I have encountered have been of Mexican descent. That is because Florida has an enormous agricultural economy. Florida has long growing seasons because of the climate. There is a large demand for temporary field workers. They will travel along the same routes as the drug traffickers. The driver or the "coyote" will load their cargo often in vans. The cargo is of course people. They will often be referred to by the traffickers as "pollos" or chickens. They will be from all parts of Central and South America. Vans are the most common means of transportation and the reason is simple. You can load more people into a single place. They are paid per person. The windows of the van behind the driver often times are very dark tinted. The driver will sometimes have another assistant who will help drive. How will you know if they are the "coyote" or the cargo? By the way they are dressed. You will see a distinct difference in the appearances in the two groups. You can see how the cargo will be dressed in much older clothes and shoes. Their luggage will most often be paper or plastic bags. They will often times appear dirty and tired. Usually they have traveled far to cross the border on foot. Once they have made it to a certain location, they will be picked up for the drive across the country. The driver is well dressed with nice clothes, shoes or boots. They will look very different from their cargo. All they have done is drive. The passengers have spent days or weeks trying to get across the border. They are immediately loaded into vans and driven for several days straight through. With this description in mind, you can get a mental picture of how different they each will appear.

To find out if the vehicle is a human smuggling vehicle, look at the rear springs. The vans would normally squat in the rear because of the weight of the people. They will put much larger and stiffer springs in the rear to prevent this. If you will go under the rear of the van you will see the added springs. Often times they are not professionally attached. You will see them with simple nuts, bolts, and clamps. The car will be cluttered with soda cans and other snack trash. Generally, the odor in the van will be strong. In many locations across the border, trying to buy a minivan is very hard. These smuggling groups will buy every one of them at auction to use.

They will charge up to $2000.00 dollars per person to transport them from the border to cities in Florida. This payment is usually made at the end of the trip. The person will be turned over to their sponsor once the payment has been made. Several times we have caught the coyotes traveling north with a large bundle of cash. This would be the transportation payments to the smugglers from the sponsors. The entire group will be turned over to the U.S. Border Patrol who will seize the persons, vehicle, and cash. As with most things in the business, after the organizations lost money several times, they quit transporting the cash. Instead, the coyotes will make regular stops and have the cash wired back to their organizations via companies like Western Union.

Several times we have caught human smuggling vehicles northbound with South American passengers. We later found out these people had lost their sponsors and were not paid for. They were now being returned back to the border. Another time in a southbound smuggling vehicle we discovered numerous females. This turned out to be part of a prostitution smuggling ring. They will pick up the young girls and take them to migrant camps throughout the state. They are originally told they are being taken for regular work. However, when they arrive to the location there will not be a sponsor. The girls are then taken to pay off their transportation debt as prostitutes. They will often earn less than $5.00 per "trick" in order to pay off their $2,000.00 cost. The Border Patrol is very aggressive with these people. The coyotes will be arrested and charged. We have many of them receiving 3-5 year federal prison terms. The passengers themselves are usually very reluctant to talk. They may want to try again to travel later or have family somewhere, which can be jeopardized.

It helps to have some basic understanding of the language of the foreign nationals you may encounter. We have taken courses in Spanish for law enforcement to help us converse better. Florida is a melting pot of cultures. Cubans who come here do not speak any English. Then there are Haitians with Creole and other Islanders who speak Patois. Patois is a combination of languages from English and African. It all depends on the various cultures you may have in your area. It pays off in huge dividends if you are an officer in the community and you practice their language. You never have to be fluent, but it helps to understand as much as you can. The people themselves are more likely to help you with problems when they see you trying to understand them and their cultures. In many parts of central and south Florida, people can go throughout their entire life without having to understand English. The communities are very tight knit and the various cultures stay together.

LABS AND THE DANGERS TO THE PATROL OFFICER - 11

I wanted a chapter to talk about labs because we need to plan about the possibilities of mobile labs. Clandestine labs possess a huge threat to us all in so many ways. There are many officers injured and disabled by this threat every month despite the controls on precursors for methamphetamine manufacture. As a patrol officer, especially in a rural area, the likely hood of encountering a lab is relatively high. Even though there are not as many lab operations in the U.S. as there once were, they are still prevalent. With new methods of cooking, the rise of the labs is again returning. Most of the meth which is utilized in the United States is transported here from south of the border. Meth produces its own set of dangers to the patrol officer. In

121

many areas of the country, methamphetamine is one of the most common drugs.

Many of these labs are mobile. Many others are broken down labs, which are being transported to a different location. There are current processes of one-pot methods where people can drive around while the chemicals are processing in the vehicle. The entire cooking method takes less than hour. It is crucial for the officer to recognize a possible lab in a vehicle. Many officers around the country have been injured by inhaling and touching chemicals they thought was something else. Common household containers are used to transport the chemicals to the lab. Many of these containers will then be taken to a location to be dumped. It is during these movements that the patrol officer commonly encounters this criminal.

In Florida, there are still many rural areas where the production of meth is practiced. This newer method like the one pot method, also called the shake and bake, is being produced because of the ease of production. The process is quite simple. Everything is placed into a single container and shaken. The pressure which is built up within the container presents explosive dangers. The containers which can be Coleman fuel cans or 2 liter soda bottles were never designed for withstanding the amount of pressure these mixtures produce. Some of the items you will see in this type of cooking method are:

- Ammonium Nitrate or Ammonium Sulfate
   - Common fertilizers
   - Anhydrous ammonia
   - Instant cold packs
- Lithium – from batteries

- Pseudo ephedrine or ephedrine pills
- Ether – Starter fluid
- Sodium Hydroxide – usually drain cleaner

The items that you may find in a standard lab can include the items below which was obtained from the Portland Oregon Police include: (21)

Acetone	Alcohol (isopropyl or rubbing)
Anhydrous ammonia and ammonium sulfate (fertilizer)	Battery acid (sulfuric acid)
Bleach	Coleman fuel
Drain cleaner (sulfuric acid or caustic soda)	Drain openers such as Red Devil lye
Heet and Iso-Heet, gasoline additives (methanol/alcohol)	
Iodine (both crystal and liquid)	Lithium batteries
Matches (red phosphorous)	Mineral Spirits
Muriatic acid	Over the counter cold pills containing ephedrine or pseudoephedrine
Salt (table or rock)	Sodium and Lithium metal
Starting Fluid (organic ether)	Toluene
Trichloroethane (gun cleaning solvent)	Hydrogen peroxide
Aluminum foil	Bed sheets

Blenders

Bottles; such as pop, water and milk bottles

Chemistry glassware

Camp stoves

Cheesecloth

Coffee filters

Cotton balls

Duct tape

Electric portable hot plates, single and double

Funnels

Garden spray jugs

Gas cans

Jugs

Paper towels

pH test strips

Plastic tubing

Pressure cookers

Propane tanks and thermos

Pyrex dishes

Rags

Rubber and latex gloves

Strainers

Swimming pool chemicals

Thermometers

Turkey basting wands

These are some of the items you may come across at a mobile lab. This is a list of items you may find in a dump site, trash can, or public trash disposal. You may also come across these items if you were to stop a vehicle that was enroute to dump them:

Rags with red and/or yellow stains

Large number of pill blister packaging from over-the-counter cold, diet or allergy remedies

Empty containers from white gas, ether, starting fluids, lye or drain openers, paint thinner, acetone, or alcohol Compressed gas cylinders, or camp stove (Coleman) fuel containers

Packaging from Epsom salts or rock salt

Propane tanks or coolers containing strong ammonia odors

Pyrex/glass/Corning containers, with dried chemical deposits remaining

Bottles or containers connected with rubber hosing and duct tape

Coolers, thermos bottles, or other cold storage containers

Respiratory masks and filters or dust masks

Funnels, hosing and clamps

Discarded rubber or latex gloves

Coffee filters, pillow cases or bed sheets stained red (used to filter red phosphorous), or containing a white powdery residue

As you can see, it may look like someone's kitchen pantry in the vehicle. You are on a traffic crash investigation and the car was left abandoned. The standard policy for most agencies will be to inventory the car and tow it for safekeeping. You open the door and there is a chemical odor coming from inside. You need to get out and move away up wind from the vehicle as fast as possible. Just inhaling small particles from some of the chemicals involved can cause lung damage. Cops are curious by nature. You see a glass mason jar in a car with a clear liquid in it; you automatically think it is alcohol. Many will open and smell the item. Do not open and smell any item you are not sure about. This could cause a lifetime of misery. Remember, in the beginning of these labs, law enforcement did not know the dangers involved with these chemicals and their byproducts. There is many, federal, state, county, and city officers who were tasked back in the early days to raid and break down these labs. They did not wear the Tyvek disposable suits and self-contained breathing apparatuses or SCBA's used today. Hundreds of these officers have since died or are completely disabled. They are suffering from complications of lung damage to rare brain cancers.

If you have a vehicle you suspect contains lab materials, as was said before, get away and move up wind. Do not let anyone near the vehicle. If your agency has a clandestine lab team, have them respond to the scene. The area needs to be cordoned off to protect anyone from getting near the vehicle. If fire rescue or other personnel arrive, be sure to notify them of the possible lab. Many fire departments have never had any training nor have experience around meth labs. Let them know that if they must approach the vehicle, SCBA's have to be worn. In most instances, because of the cost involved to clean up and dispose of a site, the DEA is contacted. They will have the personnel and resources to handle the situation. Also remember, if a subject is arrested from the vehicle, their clothes can contain dangerous chemical compounds that need to be addressed before placing them into a closed patrol car. You may have to have them strip out of their clothes before securing them in your car. A Tyvek suit or a medical gown from the medical services will suffice. Also, if your own clothes become contaminated, consider disposal of the uniform in a biohazard bag. Be sure your supervisor writes a first report of injury report for any exposures you may have had. Exposure to a chemical could have repercussions later in life. The first report of injury report will be necessary to protect you if you need assistance later on with complications to the exposure,

While we are on the topic of labs, one type has become very

126

commonplace. In Florida, there are literally thousands of indoor marijuana grows. All parts of the state have been affected. A house in almost any neighborhood can be a grow operation. Most people see these as out in the middle of nowhere grow operations. We have served warrants on multiple homes in the same neighborhood and at the same time. Not just once or twice, but all of the time.

In Florida, the indoor marijuana grow operations are mostly controlled by Cubans. Cuban criminal organizations in South Florida will purchase or rent homes throughout the state. They will then bring in Cuban immigrants and place them in the homes. They do not speak English and require little in the ways of furnishings. They are promised everything from money, cars, and even the home after they produce a certain number of crops. (22) Sometimes, they will live in the house, but usually will stay somewhere else. Generally if they live in the same house, they will seal off the area of the grow operation. Often times the grow area will be in the garage. The garage door area will be boarded off and it is common to cover it with plastic sheeting. The door to the house often times is sealed off to cut back on the odor of the fresh marijuana.

There are many hazards in a grow operation. The atmosphere itself is usually lower oxygen and higher carbon dioxide. Some try to filter outgoing exhaust with carbon filters. Others will use ozone generators in the air ducts to clear the exhaust of odor. The ozone generators produce ozone which is dangerous to inhale. Often it will be pumped into the attic which will help to dissipate the odors through the top of the roof. This will also make it more difficult for the neighbors to smell the illegal crop. Add to these items mold and chemicals throughout the house and you have a formula for disaster.

The officers who have to enter this location are in an unsafe work environment. If you are in a grow house, a good gas mask should be worn with Tyvek suits. Do not forget the maze of electrical alterations in the home. It is without question that many of these homes are a fire hazard. The electrical will be bypassed before the meter. This was their answer to law enforcement tracking electrical consumption. There will be no change to their electric bill. The additional lines will be strung all over the place in order to operate all of the equipment. Care should be taken and the local power company should be called in to secure the power.

Growing one pound of marijuana per plant about every three months, a single house can produce about $1 million a year. Grow houses ship about 100 pounds each every three months to Miami and it is then distributed in the northeastern United States, at up to $4,500 a pound.

Criminal organizations have always taken advantage of the downtrodden. In 2008, Florida led the nation in grow house bust with 1022. A spreadsheet on every grow house bust in Polk County Florida since 2005 shows that 142 of 172 suspects, or 84 percent, caught tending marijuana grow houses have identified their place of birth as Cuba. In south Florida, the percentage rate is 85-95 percent. This not a disparaging statement towards Cubans, it is just the facts. Especially in south Florida, many areas are primarily Cuban. Statistically, for the overall Cuban population it is low. Again, it is an issue of taking advantage of Cuban refugees who are recent arrivals. Is it a Cuban issue alone, absolutely not. Again, drugs are an equal opportunity employer. Because it is the worlds most abused illegal substance, anyone can be found growing it anywhere. A 200 plant grow operation was discovered in a second floor storeroom at the Mall of America in 2008 in Miami. The operators had tied into the malls power source to run the equipment. (23)

Many of these homes are discovered because of a traffic stop. So often you can smell the strong odor of raw marijuana from inside the car. The odor of the plant permeates everything the person has in their possession. Their clothes and everything in the car will smell like raw marijuana. After a traffic stop you may see things like:

Plastic plant containers, barrels, electrical wire, rolls of string, construction material, a/c duct work, electrical ballast, timers, fans, 1000 watt sodium vapor lights, rolls of plastic, fertilizers and other planting chemicals. Each light is going to need its own, igniter, capacitor, and transformers. These are a few, but not all things found at a grow operation. The possessions of these items are not against the law. However, the collection of the intelligence should be followed up upon by the proper investigative authority according to your own standard operating procedures.

THE SEARCH - 12

You have the car stopped and there are numerous things about the subjects, which attracts your suspicions. Now you want to search the car. You have removed the occupants after your backup arrives. If there are plain view items, and the laws of your state permit, you can search the car. There is nothing in plain view, but you have enough indicators to believe you should search the car. You ask for consent to search. If the owner is not present, it is generally accepted the driver can give consent. While the subjects wait outside with your back up units, you conduct the search. Just as mentioned before, I like to pat everyone for weapons. Do not let anyone use a cell phone. Remove and set aside any knives. Even if there is probable cause to search the car, I will still at times ask for consent. It gives me additional courses to conduct the search. Is it necessary to ask? No, it is just something I like to do to see what a person's reaction will be. If they say no, I explain I do not need their permission because of this or that. You will need to follow the rules of search and seizure in your state and your departmental rules.

If I have probable cause to search, I will not allow the subjects to stand around outside and watch. They are detained and need to be secured. Even if it is a completely consensual search, at times based on the number of people or weather conditions, I will have them sit in the rear of a patrol car. The windows will be rolled down and the patrol car placed closer. This accomplishes several things. Primarily, is officer safety. No one in the group can cause us any harm. The second is if they decide to withdraw the consent, they can. We are in a position we can communicate with each other. Thirdly, they are being recorded. If we are suspicious enough to search you, then we need to record you to see if you can confirm anything.

When the search of the vehicle is initiated, I have always conducted the search systematically. First, make sure the car is pulled completely off the road. Pull it even further off the road if it is possible. Start at the same point each time. Be sure to wear a good set of search gloves. Clear the passenger's compartment first. I will usually start at the right front passenger's door. This is the location I walk to on most stops so it is a natural position to start the search.

Open the door to examine the handles and lower door pocket. See if there appears to be any tampering with the inside panels or speakers. Look at all of the screws and plastic panel rivets for any signs of tampering. If there are power windows and locks, see if these switches are on a panel in the armrest. These panels can be lifted out easily, which exposes a generous void. Examine the rocker panel. Have the screws been tampered with and examine the dirt line. The dirt and dust lines are important. It shows if anything has recently been moved. If the panel has been moved, then it will be cleaner and obviously different than other areas. If the seat has an aftermarket seat cover, be sure to check under them. Always look at the bolts holding the seats for indications that a tool has been used on them. As you search the car and examine these locations, think to yourself. When was the last time I took the seats out of my car? Did you actually unbolt them from the floor? I will say it again that everything has to make sense based on your own personal experiences. False compartments in the floor below the seats are popular. In front of the hinge for the front door, there can be foam insulation, which you can push out of the way to look forward into the front fender on both sides. You may have to use a probe or baton to move it. Once these areas have been cleared, I will sit in the front passenger's seat.

Open the glove box and examine the contents. Another item we are looking for is receipts. The receipts can help confirm or discount a subject's travel itinerary. If there are any garbage or food bags on the floorboard try to locate the receipt. If it has been a long trip you will see where and when they have been. Does the trip itinerary as it was told to you match the receipts? Remove the latching system on the sides of the glove box and let it fold down. Examine the area behind the glove box and up towards the air bag. Make sure the bag is in place. You can also look a little to the left and see behind the stereo system in the dash. In this area there can be an inside air filter for the air conditioning system. Be sure to open it and look inside past the filter. If all of this is clear, check the headliner above you especially along the front edge above the windshield. It is just cardboard and you can run your fingers across the passenger's side. If there is a sun or moon roof, be sure to examine the area around it and the cover that closes it off. We have found many personal stashes in these areas. Look at the air conditioning ducts to see if there is anything visible inside. Often times you can remove the vent covers and see better inside the vents.

Look at the area of the center console. Open the console and remove all of the contents. Make sure that the plastic inside liner is secured or has it ever been removed. If there is a gearshift with a plastic or vinyl wrapped base, lift it up. Check around it and down into the console. If there are cup holders, be sure to pull these out if they are not secured. They will usually reveal a large void under the front part of the console. On the larger SUV's, the area under the center console is a very popular location to hide contraband. The console is raised because of the size of the vehicle. Generally, the entire plastic interior liner comes out and the cup holders will pull out as well. The size of the void in this area can be surprising. Stepping out of the car and kneeling down, utilize your flashlight under the seat and dash. If there is a center console, you can run your fingers under the bottom edge that covers the transmission hump. At the front edge of the console, under the dash, be sure to search this area well. There is a large void at this location and you can reach around to feel the space easily. It is a quick location for someone to stash contraband. Be sure to examine the plastic shield covering the bottom of the dash. In many models, there are simple clips for the easy removal of this plate. If you feel the search of this area is

133

complete, move on to the next location.

Next I will walk around to the driver's side and do the same examination from the open door as I did on the passenger's side. On the side of the dash is generally the fuse box cover that will remove. The horn and/or air bag cover on the steering wheel should be carefully examined. On many older models, this cover will pop off and can be a popular personal stash hiding area. Be sure to examine the driver's side floors, seat, and side of the center console. The plastic cover under the dash should be examined. We have found a handgun in this location before. Just like on the passenger's side, there may be clips for the quick opening and closing of the panel. Any pockets on the dash or above in the roof should be looked at and removed if needed. Be sure to complete the sweep of the headliner along the windshield on the driver's side. If you are satisfied, move to the driver's side rear door or pull the seat forward if it is a 2 door.

If it is a four door, again check the door areas from the outside. Lift up the bottom of the rear seat and clear this area. If someone else is assisting you, have them help you remove the seat. Look at the seat belts and see if they are passing through the slits in the seat. If not, then the seat has been removed. Once the seat has been removed, lift up the insulating padding that is covering the metal floor. See if anything appears to have been tampered with. Often times the fuel pump is located here and needs to be examined for signs of tampering. Also, the metal on the side-to-side hump at the front edge of the rear seat should be examined for any type of tampering. Often there will be small rubber caps in this area that can be removed. You can examine the void in the metal under these caps. If clear move into the seat. Lift up and check the headrest that are in front of you. Feel and check the back of the driver's seat. If it is a 2 door, check the side panel on your left closely. Also, examine the vertical plastic cover in between the driver's seat and the frame. The shoulder strap for the driver's seat belt is attached here. The molding pulls off and the area is hollow. Once you are satisfied with the search, next I will move to the trunk.

Open the trunk and examine the contents. Look to see if anything appears out of the ordinary. Is the spare tire in the proper location or is it just lying there? Remember there is a tire well or other locations for the proper tie down of the spare tire. If you do not see it, go beneath the trunk and see where it should be. There could be a false floor in the trunk. Look up at the underneath or inside portion of the trunk lid. Few people actually will look up. There are voids in the area for concealment and it usually has a carpet like covering. You should be able to tell if it has been tampered with. Look now along the edge of the trunk by the lock and see if the molding there has been removed. You can easily remove it and snap it back into place when satisfied. I will move to the sides of the trunk if it is empty. The side carpet moldings will easily pull out so you can check all of the voids leading forward above the side tire wells. If there is a lot of stuff, bags, or luggage, remove them one item at a time for examination. If there are several people in the vehicle ask them which items belong to whom. Sometimes you will have an article that no one will claim. Can you guess why? Search each item thoroughly. If it is luggage with clothes be sure to handle every piece of clothing. People love to put their drugs and paraphernalia in the socks. Be sure to examine the sidewalls of the luggage itself. If all is clear, move to the front of the trunk. If the rear seats fold down, be

135

sure to search this area with the seats folded forward. You will discover a natural cavity between the fold of the seat back and the trunk floor. A piece of carpet will cover it which can be lifted out of the way. Closely examine the speaker area beneath the hat rack. Many new upper end vehicles will have a plastic covering over the speakers. This can be removed so the area beneath the hat rack can be examined. If they have the large speaker box in the trunk, the face of the speakers can be removed after taking out the screws. Once you are satisfied with the trunk, move to the passenger's rear seat area.

Be sure to examine all of the areas as you had done on the driver's rear side. Examine the door area before going inside. As before, examine the headrest, back of the seats and sides. These include the armrest and the rear of the right front passenger's seat. Once you have completed this area, you can now move to the engine compartment.

After opening the hood, look around the engine for anything different. Watch for areas that have been touched which will leave a clean area or fingerprint. Look at the firewall for signs of tampering. Check all of the void areas in the radiator and grill. Look along the fenders on each side to make sure it appears normal. At the base of the windshield, there is a plastic molding. Most of this molding is removable with a rather large void beneath. On many models of cars, you will find the inside air conditioning filter on the passenger's side above the firewall. There will be a void beneath it. On many models, the air conditioning fan can be removed with a large void in this area. It will be obvious based on the prints which are left from taking the cover or screws off. Be sure to check the windshield washer reservoir. If still nothing is found, you can examine the tire wells and bumpers for any signs of tampering. Most people have never had their engine compartment thoroughly searched. The firewall has become a very popular location for the transportation of firearms. When you are finished with the engine, look at the tires for excessive tire weights. Look at all of the tubes and bolts that run down to the gas tank. If you will go under the car, look for areas that do not match. By not matching, I mean there will be tool marks, scratches, bolts with tool marks, under spray, or clean areas.

On different styles of vehicles, there can be other areas. Vans and mini vans will have more sidewalls to examine. Be sure to examine all of the side walls covered in plastic molding. They remove easily and have large voids behind. SUV's are notorious for having their hidden compartments in the floor from the back seat to the rear door. If you fold the rear seat forward, you will see where the floor comes up and runs toward the back at the same height. This entire area needs to be examined. Smell for the odors of glue, bondo and paint. Check the carpets for any indications of being glued down. Carpets in any location of any vehicle should not be glued. The bad guys will glue it down to keep us from lifting it up. On the SUV's, be sure to check the molding that holds down the carpet in the cargo area. Again, check the dirt line on the edge of the molding.

Pickup trucks are not very different. The area behind and beside the rear seat in the cab walls have always been very popular locations. Check the bed floor and front wall for thickness. A false front wall of the bed can be easily concealed with any type of topper. Put your hand on one side of the wall and tap the other side. You should be able to feel it. The front wall compartment will usually be through the top of the rail. The bed of the truck can have a double floor. This can usually be recognized by looking through the side of the bed above the rear tire to the other side. You should be able to see the frame, springs, and out the other side. A false floor will cover this area. At the tail gate, lower it and be sure to check the locking mechanism plate. In most trucks there will be a panel across the top of the inside tail gate. This can be taken off by removing the screws. It is supposed to be used to replace the lock, but it is a rather large cavity across the width of the gate. Look at the taillights because once removed, many will expose the inside of the side walls of the bed. The federal brake light high on the cab can be removed exposing a nice void along the roof. If there is a mounted toolbox in the bed of the truck, examine it closely. Be sure that the exterior dimensions of the box match the interior.

Is this a completed list of search locations? Of course not, but it is a good start. Let your search be guided by your intuitions. Think about where you would hide something and search it. Every vehicle will be different. Everyone has their idea of a great place to hide contraband. It is up to the imagination of the person to determine where to hide contraband. It is up to you to be just as creative and think of any type of anomaly or natural void that can be utilized.

Below is a list of locations that street users and dealers say themselves are the best places. The following list was from a marijuana user's site.

- Inside Food
- Diversion Safe – this is a common product with a false bottom like a can of flat tire fix or soda can. We have seen them as liter soda bottles or plastic water bottles. The compartment will be behind the label. Turning the bottle back and forth will reveal a

bubble for the top half and one for the bottom.

• Secret Compartment – any area in the car that can be opened

• Very Messy Trunk – This is to intimidate you to not want to look through it. The worse the better. Old food and opened condoms spread around is used to deter a search.

• Gas Tank Compartment - the gas filler door. (24)

This was found on another site for heroin abusers:

"If you are trying to conceal a small quantity of drugs, you may use your mouth, nose or ears. The mouth has the same issues we already discussed. The nose and ears have the advantage that they are not common hiding places. They have the disadvantage that if a cop decides to search in these places, there is nothing that you can do. The nose is less likely to be noticed, but it is possible to accidentally blow it out of its hiding place should you sneeze or just breath hard. It could also just fall out due to gravity. In using the ears, you must make sure that you can still hear or this will call attention to the ears. "

"For those smuggling large amounts of drugs, the anus is the typical location. There is no reason that it cannot be used for smaller amounts on a day to day basis. The reason is that in order to do a cavity search, the officer must take you into custody. This means that under normal circumstances, the anus is a very safe place to hide drugs for a short period of time. "

"Women have the advantage that they can use their vagina as a hiding place. For the purposes of this discussion, the vagina and the anus are equivalent. In either case, the drugs should be placed inside of a condom. A lubricated condom not only protects the drugs, it also

139

makes sticking it inside yourself easier and less painful. If the package is small, the condom also "bulks it up" and makes it less likely to get lost inside of you (this is surprisingly easy to do). "(25) On yet another site they are trying to teach each other what we are doing:

"This is the greatest piece of advice I have heard here yet in my short amount of time at this forum. Don't act sketchy, don't dress like a thug, practice talking to cops in situations where you can't get arrested, do plate checks on you. Failure to plan is planning to fail, and the way you dress and present yourself is the difference between a speeding ticket and "go about your business sir" and a flashing neon sign saying "search me, I have dope in the car officer!" (26) Finally here is a bunch of meth abusers and their family members telling each other where they have or can hide drugs:

I would often rollup the baggie and put it in the cap of a bic pen.

My addict boyfriend always told me (when sober) that most addicts will carry their drugs on them or have them close by.

Light fixtures under the bulbs (not screwed in all the way) to where you think the light is just burnt out.

In the plastic toilet paper roll holder (you know, with the spring in it)

Taped behind picture frames and mirrors.

In the spine of books.

Fuse box in the car or tape deck in the car.

"Stick ups"...thought they just quit smelling? No, they've been emptied and is now a hiding place.

Bottom of the Q-Tip box.

Inside of an ink pen (very common place)

Cigarette pack (very common place)

Breath mint tin, like Altoids (very common place)
Top of mini blinds
Under batteries in the TV Remote
Little coin pocket of jeans hanging in the closet

As you can see there are as many places to hide drugs and contraband as there are people. The more imaginative they are, the better the hides. Be imaginative when you are doing your search. Think like they would as you are sitting there looking at the car. Pace yourself and move slowly. Be systematic so you do not overlook anything. If someone else wants to search the car behind you, do not be offended. They will have a different set of eyes and a different imagination. You may be surprised by what they will find that you missed.

TRACTOR-TRAILERS - 13

Tractor-trailers carry a unique set of possibilities as they travel down the road. You as the interdiction officer have to look closely at all trucks. They have the potential to carry enormous amounts of all types of contraband. Just like with cars you have to consider many factors. There are thousands of tractor-trailers on the road all day every day. You have to try to select the vehicles that statistically carry the greatest possibilities for you to make an arrest. You must concentrate your attention to the owner operators. Does this mean the large companies do not transport contraband? No, of course not, they do every day. It is more likely the large companies have a dirty driver rather than the company. A trucking company can get into trouble and the next day shut the company down. They will then reopen the company under a different name. The difference will be their DOT numbers. If they are interstate carriers, they will be traveling across state lines. When they change names, they are required to change the number. That number will be higher as new companies are created everyday across the country. What is the difference between interstate and intrastate carriers? Interstate carriers operate vehicles that are authorized to operate in multiple state jurisdictions, which include U.S. and Mexican states and Canadian provinces. Intrastate carriers operate entirely within a single state jurisdiction. Based on the above definition, with the knowledge of where contraband comes and goes to, who should you be attempting to locate? If an interstate carrier can travel across state and national borders, this is where the contraband will be. When they change the company name and USDOT numbers, you can usually see the shadowing that is left behind. It can be an indicator to keep in mind at the beginning of the stop. If more things arise during the stop, it can change the course of the stop to a search.

Currently, in 2010, there are over 2,060,000 DOT numbers issued to truck companies. When you are working and see a tractor-trailer, look at the DOT number. How high the number is will tell you how new the company is. You can go to Safer web-company snapshot on any online system and get instant free information on truck companies. If you have access to the web from your patrol car, you can get instant truck company information from the USDOT numbers on the truck. Remember, the truck has to be lettered before the number with USDOT and not just DOT. Tint is another great tool for probable cause to stop trucks because they cannot have any according to Federal DOT regulations based on the high 70% visible light transmittance. The factory windows will fulfill the requirement.

If you have never worked the big trucks in your area, be sure to study up on the state and federal rules and regulations. Just like with cars, the more you know what you can do, the more you will be able to do.

My tactics for the stop of a tractor-trailer is different. Because of the size of the vehicles, I do not like the standard parking position of our vehicles. Whenever I stop a tractor-trailer, I like to follow them to the shoulder of the road just like a car. Once we are on the shoulder, I will drive along the side of the truck. I will stop in a position to the right and a little ahead of the truck and trailer. This is not possible if there is not enough area on the shoulder to drive on. If there is not enough shoulder to drive on, I may drive around and stop ahead of the truck. From this vantage point I will immediately exit my unit so I can observe the actions of the driver. A Texas DPS Trooper taught me this tactic. If you make it a standard stop for a tractor-trailer, you will pull to the shoulder at the rear of the trailer. From the back, you cannot see anything. You exit and move to the driver's side of the truck. You stand next to the traffic and wave at the driver to come back to you. The driver gets out and walks along the side of his truck back to you. While walking the 50 feet or so, the driver has traffic going past him at the roadways speed. You can stand next to the road to watch him or you can move back to the passenger's side and wait for them. As they come around the end of the trailer, you encounter him for the first time. Can you see all of the disadvantages to this tactic? It is simply terrible for both you and the driver. Remember, just as if with a car, you brought him to the stop. It is now your responsibility to get him back on the road safely. If he is a bad guy, it would be easy for him to cause you harm as he comes around the trailer. Some may say the same is true from the position in front of the truck. That is correct with several exceptions. From the front, I can see the actions of the driver. He cannot just step out and be on ground level with me. They will have to climb out and down from the truck against traffic. You have many opportunities to maintain visual observations on the driver.

We pull up just pass the right of the tractor and stop. You immediately exit and are now looking at the driver. You can also see into the cab if the curtains are open. If there is a co-driver or passenger, you have the best chance to see them now. You can also see if the driver is trying to do something different like reaching around or writing. He could be trying to hide something or change his logbook. Many of you are not DOT certified and are not comfortable with the big trucks. That's alright; you can still do your job. Truck drivers know when they get pulled over whether or not a police officer is familiar with their trade. Several things you can do from the beginning to establish yourself are to always refer to the driver as "driver." Do not look at his driver's license and call him Mr. or Mrs. so and so. It should always be "driver." It is the language they understand and respond best too. Ask them for their driver's license, registration, and medical card. They will usually get their license and medical card out of their wallet. They will generally have some type of notebook that contains the paperwork for the truck. If they are from a different state or traveling more than 100 air miles radius across the state, ask them for their logbook. 100 air-mile radius from your work reporting location can be figured as 115.08 statute or "roadmap," miles from your reporting location. (27) It is ok if you do not understand all of the time entries in the logbook. The reason you want the logbook is to see where they have been and when they were there. Ask them for their bill of lading if they are loaded. This will be their cargo manifest. Is it generally professionally printed by computer and not hand written. Most companies today operate with a computer system. Hand written bills are not as common as they once were. Some questions you may want to ask with a suspect driver are:

Who owns the truck and trailer?

How long have you driven for them?

What is your load today?

Did you watch them load it?

Who sealed the trailer?

Why are these questions pertinent? Bad companies and drivers go in and out of business. Bad drivers are always changing companies. If there are drugs in the load, they will not want to tell you that they watched it being loaded. A legitimate driver knows all there is to know about his load. His arrival on time and with a load in good condition is how they are paid. Just look at the logbook. A good driver lies about his sleep time. A bad driver lies about their driving time. Real drivers are going to drive and go over their time if they can in order to get there. Bag guys are going to be stopping with down time to get drugs loaded or off loaded. A real driver does not get paid unless the wheels are rolling. A bag guy does not care about the load. His money will be made doing something else. Remember the cost of operating a tractor-trailer. The cost can be about $0.50 per mile. They will earn about $1.00 per mile. Check the load and determine its value. Is the driver making money? If it does not make sense to you then it is probably wrong.

After a few moments have passed, it is a good time to talk to the driver about the load. He has told you that he was not there when it was loaded. There is a seal on the door. Ask if the load is on pallets, 1 or 2 stacks high, and are the locks in place. The driver answers these questions definitively; how would he know this information if he had not seen the load. The load locks will be the metal bars with rubber feet that are stretched across the sidewalls and locked in place. They keep the load from shifting back when the truck accelerates.

There are many questions to ask. These are just a few you can talk to the drivers about. Most of the drivers will be legitimate. You will know when you have a dirty driver. Spend some time stopping big trucks and get accustomed to them. Get used to talking with the drivers and one day that criminal driver will stand out to you. Their behaviors will be the same as the car drivers.

Tractor-trailers remain daunting to many of us. They really are nothing more than very big cars. An entire course can be made into the search of a tractor-trailer. Let's keep it as simple as possible. Some will say that most of the cases made from a tractor-trailer are from a discovery in the cab. In fact, I was on the border one night with the Border Patrol at the Sierra Blanca checkpoint on I-10. I spoke to the agents who told me that 85% of their seizures from tractor-trailers will be from the cab. I do not know what the national average for the concealment of drugs in a tractor-trailer is, but the cab is a good starting point. Again, no search should begin without enough back up present.

With the driver under control, step up to the passengers door. First, examine the side storage boxes, which will be used as steps. With the door open, you can quickly assess the floor and under the passenger's seat. Again, look for receipts to confirm his stated trip plans and log book. Be sure to look at the usual places on the dash like the glove box and ashtray. Be sure to look behind the ashtray and glove box. Both will pull out and you can see inside the dash. Enter the truck and be systematic. Examine the headliner and overhead pockets. Be sure to check behind the padding on the walls in the overhead storage areas which will circle the front and sides above. On the driver's side, they will often have their personal use stash in the dash or behind the horn on the steering wheel. It will usually be within arm's length of the seat. Check the closets and drawers behind the seats. Check the underneath storage of the bunk. Often times you will see a suitcase or bag in the center storage area below the bunk. Lift the bunk up and check the storage area, which runs the entire width of the cab. Watch for rolls of shrink-wrap. This could indicate that they are trying to re-wrap parts of their loads. Look at the walls, light fixtures, and air vents for signs of tampering. You will find the interior wall lining in the corners is rounded with a void behind them. Look at the headliner for any signs of tampering or tool marks on the screws.

     Moving outside again, if there is an air dam, carefully climb up and examine it. You can pull the hood forward and it will lock out. To do this, you will have to disconnect the rubber straps located on each side of the hood. There will be a foot hole in the center of the front bumper. Reach up to the center of the hood and you will find a handgrip. Pulling back on the hood with your foot in the front bumper will bring the hood forward. It will stop once it is opened and you can examine the engine compartment. Check the areas on the inside of the hood. Be sure to check the air breather. See if you can find anything that has been touched. Again, it will stand out just like a car's engine. Look at the frame under the cab and you will see a wide-open area for concealment. The battery cover can be removed and examine the batteries. There are many fake batteries on the market and I know of several cases of cocaine being found in the false bottoms of batteries. Generally, you will find two batteries. At times, they will have three or four. Remember that everything cost money. The more you spend the less you make. When you see the trucks with all of the chrome stacks, bumpers, and rims, you should be questioning how all of the extras could be afforded. According to current reports, the average driver makes $0.30 to $0.50 cents per mile. Can anyone imagine spending that much money on unnecessary equipment like chrome?

In the trailer, examine the load the best you can. If it is hot outside and you are inside a reefer unit, you will want to take along a flashlight. Have your partner close the door behind you. He does not have to lock you in, but the extreme temperature change will create a fog inside which will limit your visibility. As a safety precaution, you can place the lock through the locking plate on the driver's side door. This door will not be open during your investigation. If there is a seal on the door, do not let this prevent you from going inside. If you need to break the seal, write a note on the bill of lading that you removed it. Write seal broken by, your name, date and the department's phone number. If you replaced the seal, write the new seal number on the papers.

Once you are inside, look to see how the load is stacked. By this I mean is it on palates, or on the deck. A good legitimate load will be palletized for ease of loading and unloading. Try to look over the top of the boxes and watch for signs that someone else had walked over them. Footprints or crush areas can mean someone crawled across the load. Only two types of people will do that, cops or crooks. See if anything in the box stacks do not seem the same as all of the other stacks of cargo. Are there different types of boxes at any location or is anything not wrapped the same? Are there any high or low areas where there is something in the stack that is not like the others? Check the front wall for signs of tampering. The front wall is a very common place to conceal contraband.

You have a tractor-trailer pulled over and you work a K9 around the vehicle. The K9 alerts to the trailer. In most areas around the country, you now have probable cause to search. You do not have a K9 available so you are examining the load. It is apparent to you there is something very wrong with the load? Now what are you going to do. In either case, the load should be removed and examined more closely. Trying to plan for this eventual event can save you a lot of trouble. If you are planning to start searching big trucks, find a location where you can unload cargo if you need too. One location that has always helped law enforcement is Walmart. Speak to the managers and explain what it is you would like to do. See if you can have access to their loading dock. They have always been very cooperative. They will even have some of their dock personnel unload the trailer for you. If you do not have a convenient Walmart, go to your local grocery stores. Generally, all grocery stores are more than gracious in their assistance of law enforcement.

I know most of us will spend the majority of our time on cars, but do not overlook the trucks. Current statistics say that there are over 15 million trucks in the United States and over 2 million tractor-trailers. There are over 3.5 million truck drivers. There are another 500,000 trucks operating out of Canada. (28) There are many trucks to decide from. Work the owner operators and one day you will hit a big one.

SCRIPTS - 14

There has been a new drug business that has flourished especially in Florida. Prescription drug addiction has reached new and frightening heights. I am certain it is the same in other areas of the country as well. We are stopping vehicles from Kentucky, Tennessee and other southeastern states coming and going to Florida. We call them "pillbillies." They will either have money, prescriptions, or they will have bottles of the prescription drugs. It is a burgeoning problem in Florida because the state legislature has always refused to create tougher regulations by arguing patient privacy rights. But then the statistics continue to pour in as well as pressure from other states for Florida to toughen its laws. How do they get around the laws? Federal law states you cannot dispense prescriptions over the internet without at least one doctor office visit per year. They come to

Florida where pain clinics have flourished. They visit the doctor who prescribes the medicine. There is your one visit per year. One never realizes how bad it is until you see it in black and white.

According to the Broward County Commission on Substance Abuse of 2008, in 2007 there was a daily average of 9 lethal overdose reports in the state of Florida that involved the non-medical or illegal use of prescription medications, total of 3,317 fatal overdose reports, a 19% increase over the 2,780 fatal overdoses from the previous year. According to DEA-ARCOS reports, Florida physicians dispense five times more oxycodone than the national average of dispensing physicians. (29)   There are 89 pain clinics in Broward County alone! With a phone call to these clinics, it is discovered it is a cash-only business and they do not accept insurance. Oh yeah, they are a legitimate business. Felons run many of these businesses.

If you are not sure whether you have a prescription fraud case, here is some information from DEA, which has provided to pharmacies: (30)

Types of Fraudulent Prescriptions

Pharmacists should be aware of the various kinds of fraudulent prescriptions which may be presented for dispensing.
- Legitimate prescription pads are stolen from physicians' offices and prescriptions are written for fictitious patients.
- Some patients, in an effort to obtain additional amounts of legitimately prescribed drugs, alter the physician's prescription.
- Some drug abusers will have prescription pads from a

legitimate doctor printed with a different call back number that is answered by an accomplice to verify the prescription.

• Some drug abusers will call in their own prescriptions and give their own telephone number as a call back confirmation.

• Computers are often used to create prescriptions for nonexistent doctors or to copy legitimate doctors' prescriptions.

The following criteria **may** indicate that the purported prescription was not issued for a legitimate medical purpose.

• The prescriber writes significantly more prescriptions (or in larger quantities) compared to other practitioners in your area.

• The patient appears to be returning too frequently. A prescription which should have lasted for a month in legitimate use is being refilled on a biweekly, weekly or even a daily basis.

• The prescriber writes prescriptions for antagonistic drugs, such as depressants and stimulants, at the same time. Drug abusers often request prescriptions for "uppers and downers" at the same time.

• Patient appears presenting prescriptions written in the names of other people.

• A number of people appear simultaneously, or within a short time, all bearing similar prescriptions from the same physician.

• numerous "strangers," people who are not regular patrons or residents of your community, suddenly show up with prescriptions from the same physician.

Characteristics of Forged Prescriptions

1. Prescription looks "too good"; the prescriber's handwriting is too legible;

2. Quantities, directions or dosages differ from usual medical usage;

3. Prescription does not comply with the acceptable standard abbreviations or appear to be textbook presentations;

4. Prescription appears to be photocopied;

5. Directions written in full with no abbreviations;

6. Prescription written in different color inks or written in different handwriting.

This is from the National Institute for Health:

An estimated 20 percent of people in the United States have used prescription drugs for nonmedical reasons. This is prescription drug abuse. It is a serious and growing problem.

Abusing some prescription drugs can lead to addiction. You can develop an addiction to:

- Narcotic painkillers
- Sedatives and tranquilizers
- Stimulants

Experts don't know exactly why this type of drug abuse is increasing. The availability of drugs is probably one reason. Doctors are prescribing more drugs for more health problems than ever before. Online pharmacies make it easy to get prescription drugs without a prescription, even for youngsters. (31)

We will often stop a vehicle that has subjects from Kentucky or Tennessee. They will have one person driving and several people with various medical issues. They will tell you they were hurt in a car accident or a fall at work. They usually suffer from some type of neck or back injury. The person driving them will provide the cash they will need to take to the doctor. Often times they will have some documentation from their own doctors at home. These documents may include x-rays or MRI reports. They go to the pain management center and pay in cash. The doctor at the clinic will give them prescriptions for large amounts of the prescription drugs. This is usually oxycodone. The driver will then take the "patient" to a pharmacy and fill the prescription. They can then qualify to have prescriptions refilled via the internet. The pills bought legally cost about $5.00 to $10.00 dollars each. Taken home and sold illegally on the black market, the same pills can sell for $25.00 to $50.00 each for a 50mg tablet. There's the profit and there is your criminal.

Why should we care about this problem? My best answer is the one that hits us all in our pocket book. The diversion of controlled prescription drugs cost insurance companies up to $72.5 billion annually. Public insurers pay Two thirds of this money. You and I pay out of our pockets for this fraudulent act.

EQUIPMENT - 14

I wanted to talk briefly about some of the tools of the trade. When I first started, we did not carry any tools. After a while it was discovered that a basic tool box will be needed. We bought our own beginning tools and as time passed the department began authorizing tools to be purchased. We now carry with us an assortment of tools that we can use roadside such as:

- A basic tool box
- Regular and Phillips screwdrivers
- Standard and metric wrenches
- Socket set both metric and regular
- Cordless drill
- Allen wrenches
- Drill bits

- Brass headed hammer – for use on tapping around the tank without spark
- Regular hammer
- Portable air tank
- Pry bar or Crowbar
- Different sized probes

These are just some standard tools that we use. In addition to these we also have fiber optics, a laser measuring device (You can quickly measure the inside of a tractor's trailer) and the best and most used piece of equipment, a density meter. The density meter is the single fastest way to clear various areas of a car. You can quickly sweep over the door panels, frame, side rails and any other piece that could possibly have contraband. You can run it around the tires, over extra batteries, and anything else you may come across. Hollow items like doors and fenders will give you readings from the 20's to the 40's. Put a bundle of cash or a brick of dope inside the cavity and you will see the density measures into the 70's through the 90's. It is as simple as that. No one can completely search every cavity in a vehicle without one. Extra equipment will include an extension mirror and a camera. Photograph the scene completely from start to finish. When you know you have found contraband, photograph where it is and how you access the location. Sometimes this sounds so simplistic, yet so often it is not done. Another piece of equipment we carry in our vehicles is a fiberscope. This will give us access to view areas roadside that we may not have been able to check otherwise. You can scope out the interior of the gas tank or inside frame rails. Our newest piece of equipment is called Rapid ID. It is a very effective tool in identifying people. It is charged in our car and when needed, you can quickly scan the middle and index finger from one hand. The print is sent through the Automated Fingerprint Identification System (AFIS) for identification. If the subject has ever been fingerprinted and the prints have been submitted, they will be identified. The identification information is returned to our laptop computers. This really cuts down on false information and the identification of fugitives. Much of this equipment is available through various grants to law enforcement.

THE END OF THE SHIFT - 15

No one has ever worked this job for very long without experiencing some kind of mind numbing stress. I do not believe any discussion about this profession is complete without talking about us. At the end of the day, you go home. There is nothing out there worth taking too many risks over. Post retirement, the average life expectancy of an officer is 5-15 years less than the general population. If you intend to beat the odds, you must have a life outside of the job. All too often, I hear other officers who will say they cannot retire because they will have nothing to keep their time occupied. Speaking for myself, I can honestly tell you the job gets in the way of all of my hobbies. There is never enough time in a day for me to finish everything I enjoy. I love this job and it has fulfilled me in ways which would never have been possible in another line of work. But it is not what I live for. It is my career and I have always tried to do my best by it.

The job carries with it dangers that few have ever realized. In the Iraq war, from 2003-2009, there were 4,287 U.S. military personnel killed. There were 30,182 wounded or injured personnel. (32) Within that same timeline, there were 1,105 police officers killed in the line of duty. In addition, there were over 100,000 police officers injured by assaults alone! You see this and you have to ask yourself why this job is stressful! (33)

There are many studies out today about the stress of being a police officer. We have one of the shortest life expectancies after retirement, we have much higher divorce rates, a much higher suicide rate, and a higher than normal problem with alcohol. The why to these problems is easy. It is stress. Hans Selye, the foremost researcher of stress in the world, said that police work is "the most stressful occupation in America even surpassing the formidable stresses of air traffic control." (34) The problem is fixing it. How can you love a job so much that you allow it to kill you? The national average for divorce is 50%. For cops it is 65-75%. Our suicide rate is double the national average. Our wellness programs are some of the worse. We live, eat and sometimes sleep in a car. It is funny how interrelated the three are. Marital discord has been shown to be the number one cause of suicide in police. When the cop committed suicide there was almost always alcohol involved. Not that they were alcoholics, but that they drank that day for strength. (35)

Times are always changing and not always for the best. The respect that the job once carried is no longer there. Cynicism builds in us as the years go by because so much happens in the life of a cop,

161

which no one else understands. You are held to a different standard. In some ways I can understand that you should be held to a different standard, but inside we are all the same. We are not allowed to show the emotions and spill the pain that others are allowed. The best definition that I have found for stress is: That feeling and desire along with the ensuing bodily effects, experienced by a person who has a strong and true longing to choke the living shit out of someone who desperately deserves it, but you can't. You are held to a higher standard.

Some of the primary reasons for stress in the job are the use of your firearm, the on duty death of a fellow police officer, lack of support from your department, shift work, and dealing with the problems of the world. Everybody has a problem and who do they call? They are going to call the police. We are always there for them, but there are not many people there for us. We are held to a higher standard. We all know those older cops who have a bad attitude. One day you will all know why. There is a grind placed against you simply by the nature of the job.

Who can pull you through it? You can. You owe it to yourself and your family to take care of yourself. Mentally and physically, only you can keep the car on the road. Eat healthier, stay in a physical fitness program; spend quality time with your family. In the end, when you are tired and ready to give it all up, it will be your family who is there waiting for you. The day after you leave, the job has already forgotten you. Life goes on no matter how important you think you were. Did you make a difference? All of the things you accomplished throughout your career did make a difference to people you will never know. Someone was saved by your actions somewhere. No one may ever know this, but you. I said it at the beginning and will say it again in the end. The job entails more than most realize and produces a brotherhood that few understand. We will all feel that self-satisfaction, at the end of the shift.

NOTES

1 - http://www.fbi.gov/ucr/ucr.htm. 01Aug. 2010

2 - http://en.wikipedia.org/wiki/Police. 28 July 2010

3 - http://www.mattbraun.com/published.htm. 01 June 2009

4 - http://bjs.ojp.usdoj.gov/index.cfm?ty=tp&tid=702. 26 June 2010

5 - http://www.script-o-rama.com/movie_scripts/u/untouchables-
script-transcript-david-   mamet.html. 01 Aug. 2010

6 - http://www-fars.nhtsa.dot.gov/Main/index.aspx. 26 July 2010

7 - http://www.odmp.org/. 02 Aug 2010

8 - http://www.fbi.gov/ucr/ucr.htm. 01Aug. 2010

9 - http://www.fbi.gov/ucr/ucr.htm. 01Aug. 2010

10 - http://www.forcescience.org/. 28 July 2010

11 - F. Borelli, "Twenty-one Feet Is Way Too Close," Law
Enforcement Trainer, July/August 2001, 12-15

12 - U.S. Department of Justice, Federal Bureau of Investigation,
Firearms Training Unit, Handgun Wounding Factors and
Effectiveness (Quantico, VA, July 14, 1989).

13 -
http://caselaw.lp.findlaw.com/scripts/getcase.pl?court=us&vol=000
&invol=U20005. 04 Aug. 2010

14 - http://www.fbi.gov/ucr/ucr.htm. 01Aug. 2010

15 - http://smokingwithstyle.com/blunt_rolling.htm. 02 Aug 2010

16 - http://www.forcescience.org/. 28 July 2010

17 - http://www.batonrougetoday.com/2010/07/03/state-trooper-
shot-during-traffic-stop-on-i-10/ , 10 July 2010

18 - http://www.fbi.gov/ucr/ucr.htm. 01Aug. 2010

19 - http://www.fbi.gov/ucr/ucr.htm. 01Aug. 2010

20 - http://www.justice.gov/dea/index.htm. 03 Aug 2010

21 - http://www.portlandonline.com/police/index.cfm?c=38594. 02 June 2010

22 - http://articles.sun-sentinel.com/2009-10-30/news/sfl-florida-cuban-pot2-103109_1_cuban-drug-trafficking-organizations-growhouses-arrests. 20 July 2010

23 - http://articles.sun-sentinel.com/2009-10-30/news/sfl-florida-cuban-pot2-103109_1_cuban-drug-trafficking-organizations-growhouses-arrests . 20 July 2010

24 - http://sparkreport.net/2009/07/5-good-places-to-hide-marijuana-in-a-vehicle/. 28 June 2010

25 - http://www.heroinhelper.com/user/acquire/hiding_drugs.shtml. 28 June 2010

26 - http://www.drugsandbooze.com/showthread.php?p=325189. 28 June 2010

27 - http://www.fmcsa.dot.gov/rules-regulations/truck/driver/hos/fmcsa-guide-to-hos.PDF. 30 July 2010

28 - http://www.truckinfo.net/trucking/stats.htm. 30 July 2010

29 - Broward County Commission on Substance Abuse, United Way, 2008.

30 - http://www.deadiversion.usdoj.gov/pubs/brochures/pharmguide.htm. 11Aug. 2010

31 - http://www.nlm.nih.gov/medlineplus/prescriptiondrugabuse.html. 11 Aug. 2010

32 - http://www.globalsecurity.org/military/ops/iraq_casualties.htm. 28 Aug. 2010

33 - http://www.odmp.org/. 28 Aug 2010

34 - http://www.tearsofacop.com/police/articles/constant.html 22 Aug. 2010

35 – http://www.heavybadge.com/efstress.html 22 Aug. 2010

About the Author

Steven Varnell is a law enforcement-training specialist who retired after serving over 29 years with the Florida Highway Patrol. During his career, he worked Patrol, Field Training, Criminal Interdiction, SRT, and K9. He has instructed Firearms, Baton, Felony Stops, and Criminal Interdiction Courses. He was an adjunct instructor for the MCTFT Program at St. Petersburg College where he taught Highway Interdiction, Officer Safety, Patrol, and Interviews and Interrogation classes for law enforcement agencies throughout the country. He was a part of FHP's criminal interdiction pilot program, which began in 1983, where he served in interdiction and K9 duties for 27 year making him one of the most experienced interdiction officers in the country.

Steve is the author of Criminal Interdiction, Tactical Survival, and Behavior Analysis and Interviewing Techniques (BAIT), and Statement Analysis, An ISS Workbook, four widely acclaimed books available through bookstores everywhere. He is a sought out instructor and speaker in the officer safety field. Steve has a lecture company called Interdiction and Survival Strategies (ISS), where with former partners, together they have established a new approach to criminal based training. You can reach Steve at criminalinterdiction@live.com. For more information and training information on the ISS group, go to isspolicetraining.com.

Printed in Great Britain
by Amazon